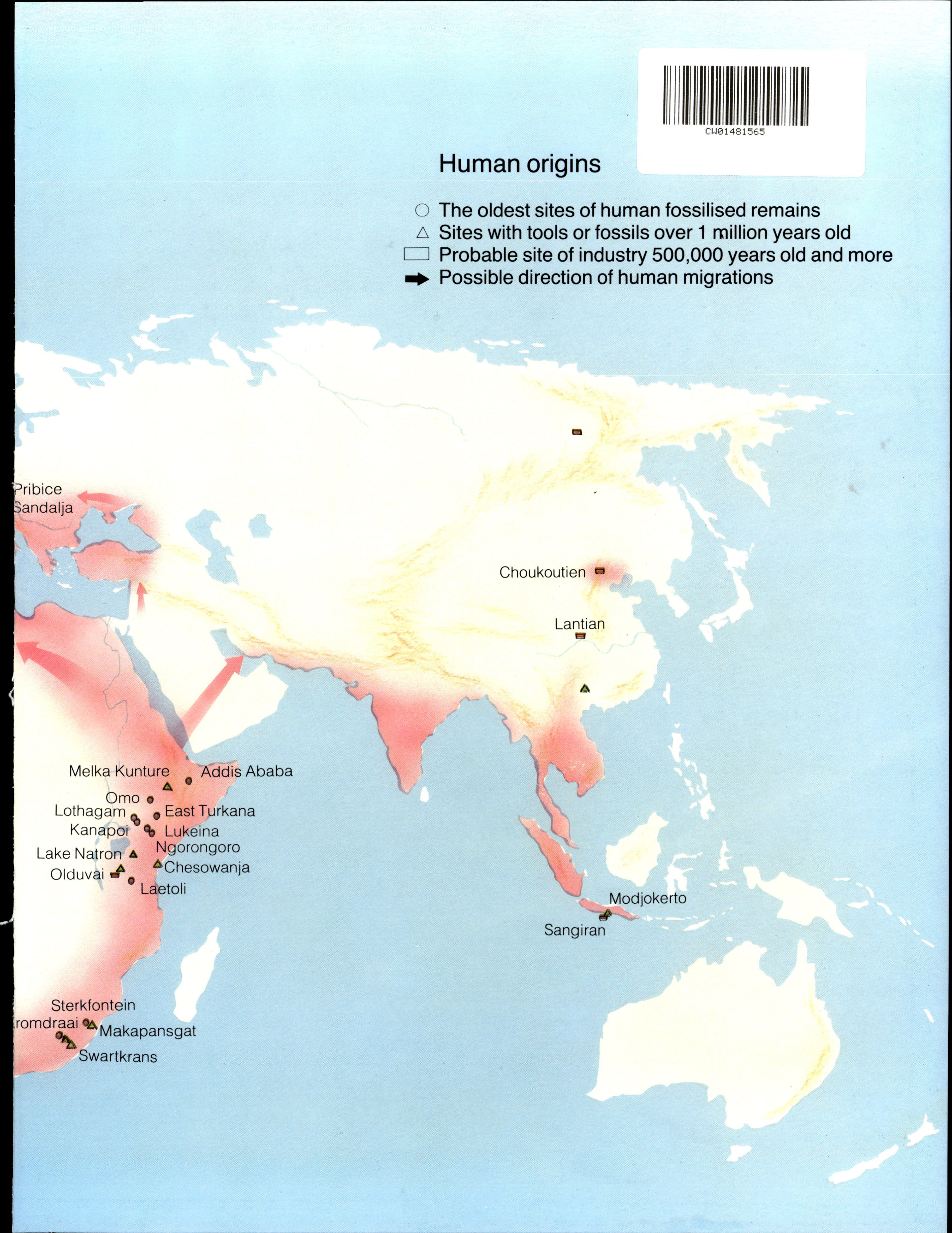

Human origins

○ The oldest sites of human fossilised remains
△ Sites with tools or fossils over 1 million years old
☐ Probable site of industry 500,000 years old and more
➡ Possible direction of human migrations

Pribice
Sandalja

Choukoutien

Lantian

Melka Kunture   Addis Ababa
Omo
Lothagam   East Turkana
Kanapoi   Lukeina
Lake Natron   Ngorongoro
Olduvai   Chesowanja
Laetoli

Modjokerto
Sangiran

Sterkfontein
Kromdraai   Makapansgat
Swartkrans

Original edition published 1986 by Casterman, Tournai
© 1986 Casterman

This edition published 1990 by Franklin Watts
© 1990 Franklin Watts

Franklin Watts
96 Leonard Street
London EC2A 4RH

ISBN: 0 86313 986 8

Editor: Jenny Wood

Picture credits
D. Serrette/M.N.H.M.: page 24. C.N.R.S.: page 28. Musée de
l'Homme: pages 41, 42 (ph. Oster), 56 (ph. de Lumley), 62 (2 ph.), 65.
Gerster/Rapho: pages 46, 66, 67b. Launois/Rapho: pages 74, 75. View
of the Sky by Alain Perceval: page 51. Lorne/Explorer: page 54.
C.N.D.P./M. Pialoux: pages 44, 58, 59. Laboratoire de Géologie du
Quaternaire – M. Taïeb: pages 67t., 72. Roger-Viollet: pages 70, 70/71,
71. Observatoire de Meudon (photos obtained by spectrograph and
computer composed by J.-M.Malherbe): pages 74, 74/75, 76.
Warren Garst for Tom Stack and Associates; pages 68, 69.

Printed in Portugal

THE HUMAN STORY

THE FIRST PEOPLE

Original text by Henri de Saint-Blanquat
Rewritten by Tim Wood
Illustrations by Catherine Nouvelle
in collaboration with
Michaël Welply and Denis Caspar

FRANKLIN WATTS

London • New York • Toronto • Sydney

CONTENTS

PREFACE

Human beings are the result of millions of years of evolution. To understand the human story, we must look at the first life-forms that occupied the planet earth. Some of them started the chain that led to the development of human beings.

Life itself was produced by the earth. Life then brought changes to the planet, since living things created the atmosphere we have today, as well as some of the rocks. So to understand anything about the basic mechanics of life on earth we need to have some idea about the beginnings of life, why this particular form of life appeared rather than any other, and why it should have done so on this particular planet.

The human story is a long one, and one that could easily have taken a different course. If circumstances had been changed only slightly, earth might have become a planet of ice or of raging heat. If there had not been a huge change in the environment 70 million years ago, the lords of earth might still be reptiles.

Life had to go through a series of remarkable developments before human beings appeared. First the great reptiles had to die out and be replaced by small, agile, furry animals that began to climb and live in trees. Then, tens of millions of years later, something had to happen for the descendants of those animals to leave the trees and walk upright on the ground. The story of the first people is a long and extraordinary one.

THE MATERIAL OF LIFE
STAR DUST

The human story begins with the creation of the sun billions of years ago, at the heart of a huge, swirling cloud in space called a nebula. Nebulae are formed of dust and gas (mainly hydrogen), and they can be billions of kilometres across. The force of gravity pulls the gases together causing the nebulae to contract at a rate of over 1,800 kilometres per hour. As the gas molecules move together, they become more tightly packed and eventually form stars. Each star takes over 1 million years to form in this way.

The movement of the molecules causes the centre of a star to become extremely hot. The hydrogen is changed to helium gas by a series of nuclear reactions. Eventually the core of a star is like a gigantic furnace, which heats up until it reaches a temperature of about 15 million°C. The huge amount of energy produced in the centre of a star would hurl the material which makes up the star out into space, if it were not for the force of gravity which holds it together. It is this balance that keeps the star the same size.

There are billions and billions of stars. The nearest one to us is our sun. It finished condensing and then burst into life about 4.5 billion years ago. The nebula which gave birth to the sun formed other stars, too. Some of these were much larger than the sun and had a much shorter life. After about 12 million years the giant stars exploded, scattering most of their material around them. This material was taken in by our newly forming sun. Most of the elements heavier than hydrogen which are found on earth and in our solar system came from the explosion of those older giant stars.

Our star, the sun, still has at least 5 billion years of life ahead of it. Without the steady flow of heat and light which it provides, life could not have developed on earth. If the sun had been just one and a half times larger than it is, it would have lasted less than 2 billion years. That would not have been enough time for life to appear on any one of its planets. We will see how the sun not only helped to create life on earth, but also how its continued existence is vital in providing the energy and food which all animals and plants need to keep them alive.

THE BIRTH OF THE PLANETS

While the sun was forming, it did not gather together all the dust and gas of its nebula around it. About one per cent was left over, and it was this material which formed the planets in our solar system.

We are not sure exactly how the planets were formed. One theory is that the material which was not drawn into the sun began to rotate around it, creating a huge, spinning disc of gas and dust. Within this disc the forces of gravity pulled the gas and dust into small knots, which in turn attracted more material to themselves. These knots then condensed to form the planets.

The planets grew larger by attracting more rocks, asteroids and smaller planetoids which were pulled gently towards them by the force of gravity. If material collided with a planet at exactly the right speed it 'stuck' to the planet, making it larger. Sometimes the approach speed was too great and the two bodies collided. When this happened, both were smashed up and the pieces drifted off in all directions, some attaching themselves to other planets and some drifting off into space. This cycle of building, destruction and rebuilding went on for about 100 million years until, eventually, the planets of our solar system were formed.

It is possible that other stars have developed their own solar systems around them. However, this could only happen if the speed at which the material rotates around its sun is exactly right. If it is too slow, the planet-building materials will not join together; if it is too fast, the forming planets will be continually destroyed. As yet, we know of no other solar system apart from our own.

In our solar system the planets and their moons gradually became fewer in number, leaving just a few loose asteroids and miniature planets drifting around. As they spun, the planets heated up but because they were much smaller than the sun, they never became hot enough to burst into flames in the way that stars do.

While this planet building was going on, the sun continued to form. We know from the age of the rocks which occasionally fall on to the earth in the form of meteorites, that our whole solar system is about 4.5 billion years old. It would have been fascinating to watch these gigantic lumps of rock being pulled towards each other, gently merging and then becoming round through the effects of gravity, as the newly formed planet spun on its axis. But this process took place billions of years before human life appeared and the silent, lifeless meteorites were the only witnesses to the birth of our solar system.

No one has ever seen the birth of a planet, so any ideas about how planets form can only be theories. The most generally accepted theory to explain the birth of our solar system is that the planets were formed from a gigantic spinning disc of gas and dust. The forces of gravity in this disc caused the gas and dust to merge, so that the planets grew in the same way that a snowball rolling down a snow-covered hill grows larger.

OUR SOLAR SYSTEM

The planets in our solar system vary enormously. Mercury spins so slowly that one day there lasts for 176 earth days. On the other hand, Jupiter spins so fast that one day there lasts for less than ten earth hours. A day on Mars lasts 26.4 earth hours, but its year is nearly twice as long as ours.

The planets' landscapes are very different, too. There is a crater 1,300 kilometres in diameter, a little to the north of the Equator on Mercury, which is the result of a colossal collision with a gigantic meteorite about 3.8 billion years ago. Mars has four giant volcanoes up to forty-two kilometres high, and a huge canyon about 7,000 metres deep and 5,000 kilometres long.

If you were to stand on Io (one of Jupiter's moons), Jupiter would seem to fill the sky, appearing ninety times bigger than our moon does when seen from earth. Above you would loom the Great Red Spot (a gigantic hurricane which can always be seen in Jupiter's atmosphere) and the famous belts – long, brown, cloudy bands. You would just be able to see the sun, 778,000 million kilometres away. It would appear as a tiny, bright star.

Unfortunately, it seems that earth is the only planet in our solar system which has the right conditions to support life. The temperature on Mercury varies from 400°C in the day to minus 170°C at night, and there is no atmosphere to breathe. The surface temperature of Venus is about 470°C, and although the planet does have an atmosphere it is mainly carbon dioxide. Many hoped that when the American space probe *Viking* landed on Mars, where the temperatures are less extreme and there is a thin carbon dioxide atmosphere, it would discover signs of life. Sadly, this was not the case.

In fact Titan, a large moon of Saturn, is the only other body in our solar system which might, in the far distant future, support life. Titan is slightly bigger than Mercury and has an atmosphere. Admittedly the temperature is about minus 178°C and the ground is covered with an ocean of liquid methane, but the atmosphere is mainly nitrogen, like earth's. It also contains hydrogen cyanide, which scientists believe must be present if life is to start. However, it will take several billion years for anything to develop, so, meanwhile, the only life we know about in our solar system is on earth.

Our solar system. Working out from the sun you can see Mercury; Venus; Earth and its moon; Mars; Jupiter with four moons (Io nearest); Saturn with its rings and moon, Titan; and Uranus. Neptune and Pluto, which are further out, are not shown.

THE PLANET EARTH

The earth, which is slightly younger than the sun, was born roughly 4.48 billion years ago. At the start of its life, earth was a fiery ball of molten (liquid) material floating through vast clouds of rocks, gas and dust, and attracting much of this material to itself by the force of gravity. As the planet cooled it began to shrink. Soon the various layers of the earth began to appear. The outer part, the surface, cooled first and formed a thin crust of rock. Beneath the crust lay a mantle of molten rock. Under the mantle the heaviest elements, such as nickle and iron, sank to the centre of the planet, where they formed the core.

For about the first billion years of its life the earth was an inhospitable place. Its surface was pitted by thousands of volcanoes which belched out molten rock, ammonia, methane and carbon monoxide. The planet's unstable crust, constantly on the move as it floated around on the red-hot mantle, was torn by earthquakes. It heaved and buckled under the colossal stresses and strains caused by the earth cooling and shrinking. It split as chunks of the heaviest elements, such as iron, broke off and sank into the fiery depths.

The crust was also scarred by showers of meteorites which constantly bombarded the earth. Most of the craters these caused disappeared during the upheavals of the crust, but huge chunks of meteoritic rocks and minerals still lie under the surface of every continent, particularly in southern Africa, Canada and the Soviet Union. Scientists believe that several meteorites found in Egypt and Antarctica came from Mars about 1.4 billion years ago. This means that the growing planet Mars must have been struck by something with enough force to throw these rocks out of its field of gravity. Another piece of rock found in Antarctica seems to come from the moon. In fact, some people believe that the moon itself is an enormous piece of the earth, torn away by a planetary collision.

This turbulent period in earth's history lasted a comparatively short time. By about 4.45 billion years ago earth had an atmosphere, though it was very different from the one we breathe today, since it was made up mainly of water vapour, ammonia and methane. It also had an ocean, although this was acidic and very hot. By about 4 billion years ago the core had settled down and, as a result, the crust stabilised and the mantle became more solid. Earth had an atmosphere, oceans and the beginnings of landmasses. All it needed now was rain.

AN EARTH WITHOUT LIFE

Earth is the only planet in our solar system on which we *know* that life exists. Scientists now believe that life probably does exist only on earth, and that it came about through a unique set of circumstances.

The first essential development was the creation of an atmosphere. On earth this happened as the planet cooled. The water vapour, ammonia and methane which had been present in the dust of the nebula were squeezed out from the centre of the planet to create an atmosphere around it. Ultraviolet rays from sunlight began to warm the atmosphere. This heat was trapped by the blanket of cloud around the earth, creating a 'greenhouse effect'. As a result, much of the ammonia and methane were broken down into simpler chemicals. This left a new atmosphere which was made up of hydrogen (most of which escaped into space), and nitrogen and carbon dioxide which fell with the rains into the newly forming oceans. Together they formed a kind of chemical soup from which life evolved.

Venus, earth and Mars are sister planets which must have started out in fairly similar situations. All three planets must have developed atmospheres, yet life appeared only on earth. On Mars the greenhouse effect created enough water for rain, rivers and even shallow oceans. Then the greenhouse effect faded. The water became ice and is now found only at the planet's two poles. The small amount which melts in the summer is not enough to provide the permanent supply of water which life needs to exist.

Venus received more heat from the sun, but its atmosphere also contained more carbon dioxide. This created heavy clouds which trapped the heat and increased the greenhouse effect. As a result, its water quickly evaporated and the ground temperature rose dramatically.

Some greenhouse effect is needed to form life, but too much will kill it. If the earth had been 142.5 million kilometres nearer the sun, the planet would have become hot like Venus. If the earth had been 151.5 million kilometres further away from the sun, the planet would have become covered in ice like Pluto. Fortunately, as the continents formed, most of the carbon on earth became trapped in the rocks rather than escaping into the atmosphere. This lessened the greenhouse effect. Earth also escaped being frozen over, although at certain periods in the past this has nearly happened. By lucky chance our planet was correctly placed to avoid becoming either too hot or too cold. As a result, life was able to develop on earth.

LIFE BEGINS SLOWLY

At first, earth's atmosphere was poisonous. It was made up of gases such as hydrogen, nitrogen, methane and carbon dioxide. It also contained some water vapour, but no oxygen. For millions of years these chemicals were heated by sunlight and by erupting volcanoes. Electric storms raged through the atmosphere. The lightning and the heat reacted with these gases, and 'cooked' them to produce simple molecules of sugar and amino acids, the basic building blocks of life. Over millions more years, these molecules joined together to form more complicated molecules which eventually became the first living things.

In 1953 two American scientists, Stanley Miller and Harold Urey, did experiments to recreate this process. They filled a flask with ammonia, hydrogen, methane and water, then passed electric sparks similar to lightning through the mixture. After a week they found that the mixture contained amino acids and sugar. Other experiments have shown that when amino acids are heated, long chains of molecules appear. These molecules are very similar to those which make up various living tissues, such as blood and skin.

The first living creatures were probably produced by the action of heat and lightning on the poisonous chemicals of the atmosphere about 3.2 billion years ago. These first creatures were tiny and looked rather like microscopic bacteria. These bacteria slowly developed into a sort of blue-green algae (the simplest form of plant life) made up of a single cell with no centre, or 'nucleus'. The algae, which joined together into large colonies called reefs, could photosynthesise. This means that they had the ability which all green plants have to take energy from the sun and turn it into food for themselves, while releasing oxygen into the atmosphere.

For over 2 billion years these algae were the only form of life on earth. Although they were so small and so simple, they gradually transformed earth's atmosphere, converting it from a deadly mixture of poisonous gases into breathable oxygen. However, it was not until about 650 million years ago that the first kinds of more complicated creatures appeared. These were mostly types of jellyfish, corals and worms which lived, like all early creatures, in the seas. From that moment, the development of life began to speed up, although millions of years were to pass before the first vertebrates (animals with backbones) appeared.

THE CELL

All living things are made up of cells. Some animals and plants consist of only one cell, but more complicated life-forms may contain billions of cells. Most cells are so small that they can only be seen under a microscope. About 500 average-sized cells would fit on to the full stop at the end of this sentence.

In spite of being so small, a cell is amazingly complicated. Each cell can be a complete world, even a universe. A single white blood cell, for example, contains a billion molecules. Some single-celled plants and animals can lead independent lives. More complicated animals and plants have many cells. Some of these adapt to perform special tasks. In animals, for instance, some cells adapt to become muscle cells or nerve cells.

All cells are alive. They breathe, take in food, get rid of waste, grow, reproduce and eventually die. Each cell is surrounded by a thin case, or membrane. Inside this is a jelly-like fluid called cytoplasm which contains many tiny structures, each of which has a particular job to do. The most important of these structures is the nucleus, which is the control centre of the cell. It contains the cell's genetic programme, a master plan which controls everything the cell does.

Cells reproduce themselves by splitting to create two new cells. Each new cell gets a copy of the genetic programme. Animals pass on their characteristics to their offspring because these characteristics are contained in their cells. However, sometimes the genetic programme is slightly changed, possibly because of some damage. This means that the offspring is slightly different from its parents. Over millions of years, these changes, or 'mutations', can produce completely new creatures. If the change makes the animal less able to survive, it will not breed successfully and its mutated children will die out. If the change makes the animal better able to survive, it will pass on the improvement to its offspring. This process of gradual change and improvement in animals and in plant life is called evolution.

This is a cell seen through an electron microscope. It is in the process of swallowing up another cell. Cells can divide and produce two identical cells. It is this continual division that allows a fertilised human egg to be transformed gradually into an embryo, then into a foetus and finally into a baby which grows and develops into an adult.

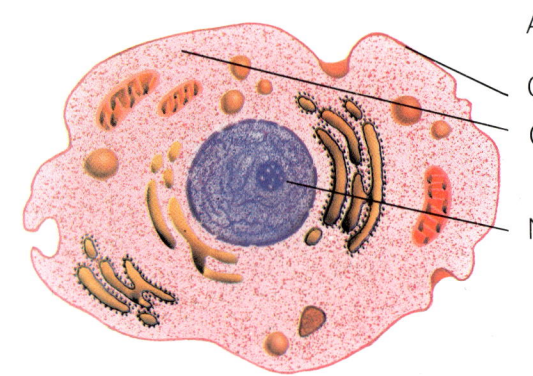

AN ANIMAL CELL

Cell membrane

Cytoplasm

Nucleus

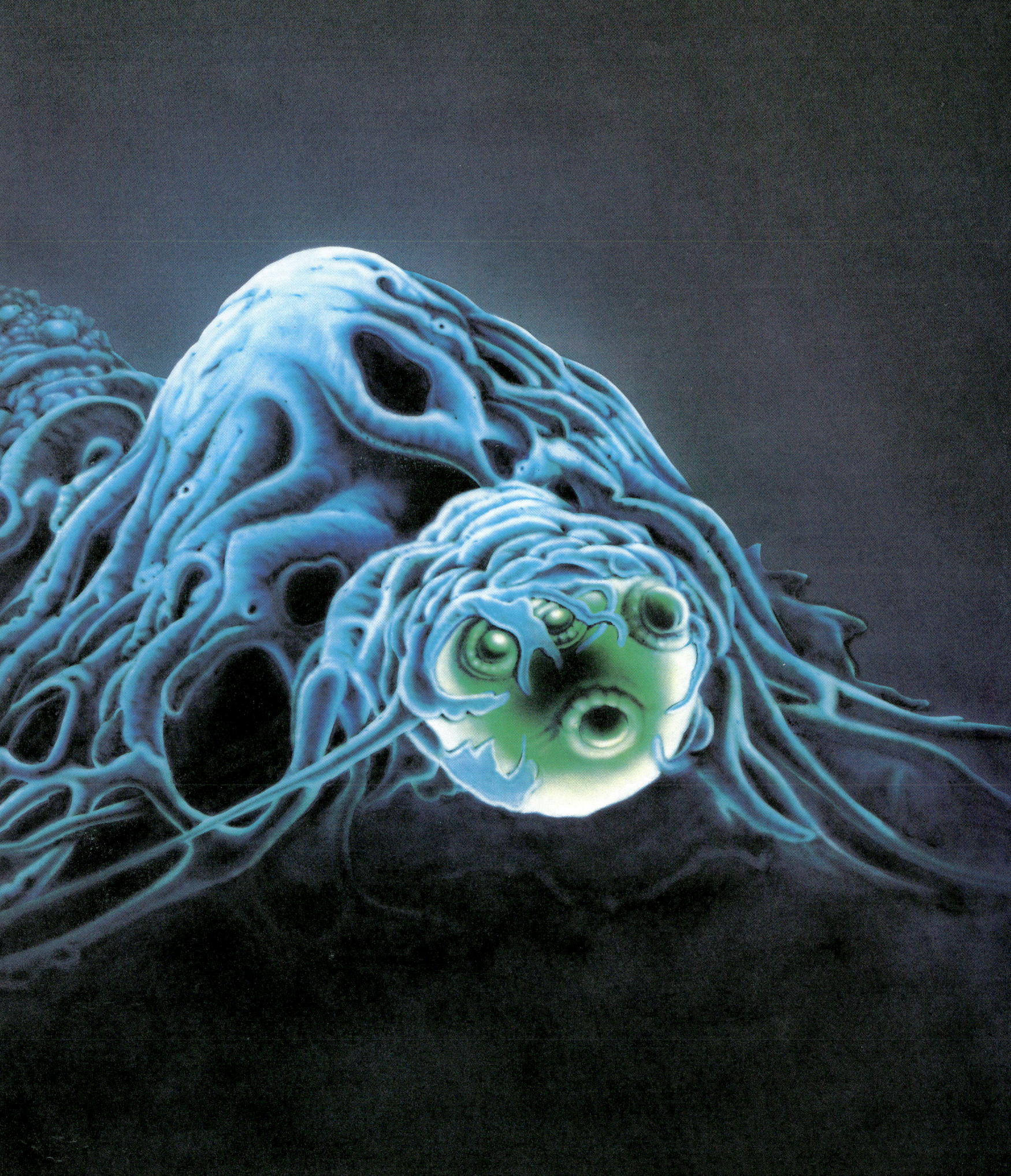

THE FIRST ANIMALS
THE FIRST SEA CREATURES

By the beginning of the Palaeozoic era (about 600 million years ago), the earth had already existed for 4 billion years. Although living cells had been around for 3 billion years, the development of animals had been very slow. The creatures at that time were all very simple ones which lived in the sea. They had no brains, no stomachs, no hearts, no fins and no lungs.

However, during the early part of the Palaeozoic era, animals began to evolve more rapidly. This process may have been started by chemical changes in the sea water which allowed calcium to harden into bones and shells. As a result, the first creatures with shells or bony skins began to appear. Some of the earliest to develop were molluscs, sea urchins and trilobites. Some of these early armoured creatures, such as the trilobites, are related to insects.

Gradually some of these animals developed backbones to protect their spinal cords. These creatures, which appeared about 500 million years ago, had eyes, mouths, gill slits, and bony armour which protected the fronts of their bodies. They were the ancestors of a long line of new animals called vertebrates, a family to which we humans belong.

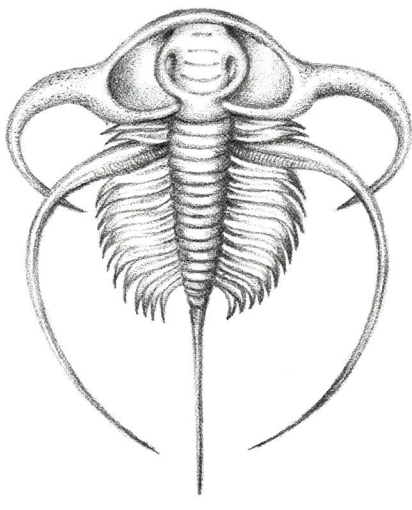

A trilobite. We know that there were thousands of different kinds of trilobites alive in the Palaeozoic era because of all the fossils which have been found. They probably ate tiny sea creatures called plankton and may have rolled themselves into balls when attacked, rather like wood lice do today.

Fish with bony armour, gastropods which are distant cousins of snails, and crinoids, which are related to starfish and sea urchins, swam in the Palaeozoic seas.

Many Palaeozoic fish had armour plates on the front parts of their bodies. Only the back parts were left unprotected. Here a gigantostracans, a distant relation of the scorpion, uses its large claws to attack the soft body of a slow-moving fish.

FOOTSTEPS IN THE MUD

Most of the Palaeozoic fish breathed through gills as they swam through the sea. However, one group of fish developed a new way of breathing and moving. They are known as lobe-fin fish, because their fins were supported on fleshy lumps called lobes. It was these creatures which were the first to move out of the sea and on to the land.

In the middle of the Palaeozoic period the seas started to retreat, leaving many lobe-fins stranded in newly formed lakes. They used their strong front fins to crawl along the lakes beds looking for food. They were able to survive in very shallow water, close to the air, because part of their stomachs developed into lungs. Gradually, tempted by the insects which flew about over the land, these lungfish began to crawl on to the shore.

Lungfish still exist today, although they do not move around much on land. When the water in their pools dries up, they bury themselves in the damp mud and wait for the water to return.

The first amphibian (a creature that can live both on land and in the water) was *Ichthyostega*. It first crawled on to the land about 345 million years ago. Each of its limbs, which ended in five, small toe-like bones, was more like a leg than a fin. Over millions of years these fins developed into proper legs. As the only large creature on the land, *Ichthyostega* had no enemies and so could sleep in peace without fear of attack. It lived in the swampy lagoons of the Palaeozoic era, hunting on land, and returning to the water from time to time to keep its skin damp and to breed.

Reconstruction (about 0.5m long) of a lungfish of the Devonian period.

A modern-day Australian lungfish (about 1.5m long).

The fossilised imprint of a fern. Ferns were already growing before the Palaeozoic period.

This is what Greenland may have looked like 350 million years ago. *Ichthyostega*, the first amphibian, is emerging from the marshy lagoon where it lives. It moves among the grass and ferns, some of which are as big as trees, hunting for spiders, millipedes and scorpions.

This shows how a lobed fin (1) may have developed into the leg of an amphibian (4). Notice how the bones grow larger and the foot turns downwards to support the creature's weight. The sixth and seventh toes in (4) disappeared about 300 million years ago, to leave a five-toed foot.

THE TERRIBLE LIZARDS

The amphibians were not true land animals. They had to return to the water to mate and to lay their eggs. Their skins were not waterproof, so they dried up and died if they spent too long on land. During the Permian period, about 250 million years ago, the weather was very hot. The amphibians, which up to then had dominated life on land, were unable to stand the heat. They became extinct or were driven back into the water where, in many cases, their legs became feeble and useless. Their place was taken by another group of creatures who were able to live on land all the time. These were the reptiles.

During the Mesozoic era, the most successful reptiles were the dinosaurs. Dinosaurs had waterproof skins so, unlike the amphibians, they could live in hot areas away from lakes and rivers. In fact, the warm climate suited the dinosaurs perfectly because many of them were cold-blooded and could not control their own body temperature. They needed the hot sun to warm their bodies and make them active.

Dinosaurs also had a new kind of egg. These contained amniotic fluid, which provided a food supply for the growing body. The eggs also had waterproof shells, which meant that the animals could lay them on dry land.

There were two main kinds of dinosaurs: the herbivores, which ate plants, and the carnivores, which ate meat. They came in all shapes and sizes. Some of the herbivores were as big as buses and lumbered along on four legs. Many developed horns, spikes and armour to protect themselves from the carnivores. Many of the carnivores were descended from small, fast dinosaurs which ran along on their two back legs.

The dinosaurs dominated the land for over 150 million years. They came in all shapes and sizes. the most fearsome of the carnivorous dinosaurs was *Tyrannosaurus rex*. It was over 14m long and stood over 5m high.

Stegosaurus

Brontosaurus

Coelophysis

Ornitholestes

Iguanodon

Parasaurolophus

Anatosaurus

Triceratops

Lambeosaurus

Strunthimimus

Tyrannosaurus rex

C·N

STEGOSAURUS AND OTHERS

Throughout the history of the dinosaurs, there was constant competition between the carnivores and the herbivores. As the flesh-eaters, or carnosaurs, grew bigger, so did some of the plant-eaters. Among the biggest were the sauropods. *Diplodocus* was about twenty-five metres from tail to snout and stood about thirteen metres high when it stretched out its long neck. *Brachiosaurus* was even bigger. It measured about forty metres from nose to tail, and weighed up to eighty tonnes. It was the biggest land animal that ever lived, only slightly smaller than the 100-tonne blue whale, which is the largest sea creature. The huge bulk of the giant sauropods was probably their best defence against the carnosaurs. Even today few animals will attack an animal as large as an elephant.

Other herbivores called ceratopsians, such as *Styracosaurus* and *Triceratops*, developed horns and bony neck shields which protected their heads and necks. Ceratopsians probably used their horns for defence against carnosaurs. They may also have used them for fighting against each other, rather like stags do today. The last of these living tanks was about nine metres long and over four metres high. In spite of their ferocious appearance, they ate only plants. They had parrot-like jaws, armed with long teeth which slid up and down against each other like shears, slicing and chopping through tough stems.

Other dinosaurs, such as *Stegosaurus*, developed triangular armour plates which ran down the length of their backs. *Stegosaurus* had a powerful tail which ended in large, sharp, bony spines. It may have swung this tail like a gigantic club. Some scientists think that the back plates may have had another use, as a kind of radiator. In cool weather they may have lain flat on the creature's back to collect more of the sun's heat, while in hot weather they may have stood upright to help the dinosaur lose heat from its enormous body.

Although thousands of dinosaur fossils have been found in many different parts of the world, there is still much which is unknown about them. Experts called palaeontologists, who study fossils, still argue fiercely about the habits of these magnificent creatures. Some think that dinosaurs may not all have lived in marshy areas, and that they were much more agile and swift than is generally believed. It may even be possible that some dinosaurs were warm-blooded. Whatever the case, these 'terrible lizards', as they are sometimes called, ruled the earth for over 150 million years.

Dinosaur footprints fossilised in the African mud. Footprints like these have been found all over the world and help scientists to measure the length of a dinosaur's stride.

Although the dinosaurs were one of the most successful groups of animals, they were not very clever. A typical dinosaur brain was about the size of an apple. *Stegosaurus* had a second brain near its hips which may have controlled its club-like tail. *Stegosaurus* was a very successful creature which survived for about 100,000 years.

THE CONQUEST OF THE AIR

The first flying reptiles, called pterosaurs, appeared about 160 million years ago and were related to the dinosaurs. One of the earliest pterosaurs was *Dimorphodon*. It looked very similar to its dinosaur ancestors, with a short head and long, sharp teeth. Unlike its land-living relations, however, it had many hollow bones which made it light enough to fly. Its wings were a leathery membrane stretched between its back legs and the very elongated fourth fingers of its front legs.

As time went by, the skulls of the pterosaurs became longer and narrower, while their tails grew shorter. Eventually their teeth were replaced by horny beaks. One of the last, *Pteranodon*, had no tail, so it must have moved its head to steer, using the long crest on its head as a rudder. It had a wingspan of about eight metres and probably soared out over the ocean, like an albatross, diving for fish and storing the catch in its beak pouch, rather like a pelican does.

Pterosaurs could only flap their wings feebly, so they were not strong enough to fly properly. It seems likely that they were expert gliders, using the air currents to support themselves. On the ground they could only hobble about clumsily, dragging their wings along. Many of them may have lived in colonies on high cliff faces where they would have been safe from carnosaurs.

As the pterosaurs glided along, the flow of air across their bodies must have cooled them rapidly. Some scientists believe, for this reason, that the pterosaurs may have been warm-blooded and so were able to regulate the temperature of their own bodies. Fossil evidence certainly proves that some pterosaurs were covered in fur.

The pterosaurs did not have the skies all to themselves. Eventually they were joined by *Archaeopteryx*, the first creature which could be described as a true bird. It looked similar to the flying lizards, with two important differences. These were a wing skeleton, formed from its long claw bones, and feathers. *Archaeopteryx* was probably warm-blooded and, since it could probably flap its wings like a real bird, was a stronger flyer than the pterosaurs.

By the end of the Mesozoic era, a number of different birds had developed powerful wings and could fly long distances. Some had webbed feet and obviously spent much of their time on the water, swimming and diving for fish.

At the time when the pterosaurs and the earliest birds were making their first clumsy flights, the air had already been buzzing with insects such as giant dragonflies and mayflies for 100 million years.

Pteranodon

Dimorphodon

Rhamphorhynchus

Archaeopteryx

Hesperornis

Icarosaurus

C.N

THE END OF THE DINOSAURS

The fate of the dinosaurs is one of the greatest mysteries in nature. For 150 million years they seemed to evolve quite normally. By the end of the Cretaceous period (130 million years ago), there were hundreds of different types. It seemed that dinosaurs would rule the earth for ever.

Then, over a period of only a few million years, the dinosaurs and their cousins, the pterosaurs, became extinct. Many other creatures, such as ammonites and belemnites, which lived in the sea but were not reptiles, died out as well.

No one knows why this happened, although scientists have put forward many theories. One possibility is that the dinosaurs were unable to compete with a new creature, the mammal, which stole their eggs. Another idea is that a major catastrophe, such as a gigantic volcanic explosion, or a collision with a huge meteorite, may have caused a world-wide disaster such as a major change in the weather.

What we do know is that great changes took place on the planet. Until then, much of Europe had been under water and most of the world had had a warm climate. However, at the end of the Cretaceous period the sea level dropped by over 200 metres. Scientists are still trying to work out why this happened. New research shows that volcanic eruptions can have an important effect on the climate of the whole world. A period of increased volcanic activity might have thrown millions of tonnes of ash into the atmosphere and increased the cloud cover around the world. This in turn could have led to a drop in world temperatures. A long period of cold weather would have had a devastating effect on the cold-blooded dinosaurs.

As the sea level dropped, we can guess that the increase in the area of land made the climate colder and drier. The warm, shallow waters around the land became deeper and colder, too. Creatures that needed warm water and warm weather to survive died out in their millions. The colder climate was like a death sentence.

This 'great dying' was one of the most widespread and terrible destructions in the history of living things. The planet was almost emptied, although some fish survived, as did the warm-blooded birds and some small, shrew-like mammals. Although it would take millions of years to happen, these mammals which had been greatly outnumbered by the reptiles eventually filled the empty place left by the mysterious passing of the dinosaurs.

As the dinosaurs began to disappear, large, flightless birds such as the *Diatryma* took over the job of the carnosaurs. These birds, which were over 2m high, soon died out, destroyed by the first carnivorous mammals. Some even larger birds of this type developed much later and lived in South America.

THE BIRTH OF THE MAMMALS

Mammals first appeared during the Mesozoic era. In the beginning, all mammals were small creatures which looked rather like shrews. There were three main groups: the insect eaters, which later developed into the rodents and bats; the ungulates, which evolved into the large mammals; and the primates, which became the apes.

Unlike reptiles, the warm-blooded mammals were able to survive in cold climates. They had a number of advantages over other animals, which helped them to conquer the earth. One of the most important was their method of having babies. Most amphibians and reptiles laid dozens of eggs, many of which did not hatch or were eaten by predators. Mammals, on the other hand, gave birth to live young. This meant that the mammal mother could protect her baby right up to the moment of birth. It was much easier for a predator to steal a reptile egg than it was to kill an adult mother. So although mammals had fewer young than the reptiles did, the mammal young were much more likely to survive.

Mammals had many other advantages over earlier creatures. Mammal mothers fed their young with milk. While they did this the baby was protected by, and learned from, its mother. As a result, mammal brains grew larger. The fur which mammals grew protected their bodies from the cold which had probably helped to kill off the reptiles. Mammals had better jaws and teeth, stronger lungs which helped them lead more active lives, and a good sense of smell. Helped by these advantages, the mammals began to spread all over the planet, gradually taking over the vacant areas which had been left by the death of the dinosaurs.

Although the mammals began as very small creatures, some of them grew to enormous size, nearly rivalling the dinosaurs. The largest was *Baluchitherium*, a kind of rhinoceros which lived 30 million years ago. It was over eight metres long, and its head towered over five metres from the ground. Twenty million years later, a kind of giant llama was eating leaves from branches over eight metres high.

Around 14 million years ago, giant versions of modern animals such as sloths, armadilloes and anteaters were living in South America, while mammoths and elephants roamed across Europe and Asia. Of course, the largest of all the mammals were the *Cetaceans*. This group includes the blue whale, the largest creature that has ever lived. It grew much larger than even the biggest dinosaurs such as *Brontosaurus*.

The first mammals were very small, and were overshadowed by the big reptiles. When the dinosaurs disappeared, some mammals grew very large. Here you can see some of the biggest. *Alticamelus* (back) was a cross between a camel and a giraffe, and lived about 20 million years ago. *Baluchitherium* (centre) lived in Asia 25 million years ago. *Megatherium* (front) was a giant sloth which lived in South America about 60 million years ago.

THE BEGINNING OF HUMAN LIFE
THE PRIMATES

It took something like 60 million years for mammals to develop from the first shrew-like creatures into animals as different as bats, elephants, gazelles, hyenas and primates. This is a remarkably short time compared with how long it took for the first reptiles to appear. Evolution had started to speed up.

The group of mammals to which humans belong is called the primates. Primates all have five fingers and toes, so their hands, and often their feet, can be used for grasping objects. They all have forward-pointing eyes which helps them to judge distances very well. Many primates have large and complex brains and are among the most intelligent of all animals. Most of them live in family groups, or even in small 'tribes'. Some primates have learned how to use sticks and stones as primitive 'tools'.

Primates developed into four main groups. The prosimians, the oldest group, are animals which, as their name indicates, are not quite apes. This group includes the lemurs of Madagascar which are nocturnal, live in trees and eat fruit. They have huge eyes to help them see in the dark, and 'prehensile' tails which can grasp tree branches. Some prosimians, such as the tarsier which now lives in the islands of the Philippines, developed a thumb which could grip objects well.

The second group, the New World monkeys, were primates which were trapped in South America when the continents drifted apart. They developed in slightly different ways from primates in other parts of the world, having broad, flat noses with the nostrils far apart, and grasping, or 'prehensile', tails. The spider monkey, the howler monkey and the marmoset are all members of this family.

The third group, the Old World monkeys, lived in Africa and Asia. Their nostrils are close together and open to the front. They do not have grasping tails. They have larger brains than the New World monkeys. Some, such as the proboscis monkey of Borneo, the African colobus and the Asian macaques, live in trees. Others, such as the baboons of eastern and southern Africa, live on the ground.

The anthropoids were the last group of primates to evolve. They appeared about 20 million years ago. Included in this family were the large apes, such as the orangutan, the gorilla and the chimpanzee. Anthropoids have large brains and no tails. It was members of this group that, after millions of years, evolved into human beings.

The common ancestor of all the primates may have been a shrew-like creature like this.

There are over 150 species of primates living today. You can see examples of all four groups here. The word primate means first. It is used to show that members of that family belong to the most advanced stage of evolution.

Tarsier

Lemur

Baboon

Macaque

Marmoset

Silky tamarin

Gorilla

Chimpanzee

Human

APES AND HUMANS

It is quite wrong to think that humans descended from apes. The truth is that, at some time in the distant past, apes and humans shared a common ancestor. Unfortunately we do not know exactly when or how the ancestors of humans, the hominids, developed in a different way from the apes. Many of the most important links in the fossil record which would tell us the complete story of our own evolution from apes to humans is missing.

Some scientists believe that one of these missing links might be a creature called *Ramapithecus*. They believe that this was the first ape which came down from the trees and lived on the ground. The creature had some human features, especially in the jaws and teeth. It may have used its hands to pick grass seeds and then eaten them sitting on the ground. Its most important feature was that it developed the ability to walk upright on its hind legs.

Other scientists believe that there must have been one or several human ancestors which came before *Ramapithecus*. They think that these creatures would have had much in common with chimpanzees and orangutans, whose genetic programmes are quite similar to those of humans. Unfortunately no fossil remains of any such creatures have yet been found, so the story of our early ancestors has to remain incomplete for the moment.

There may have been many different types of human-like apes which came down from the trees to try out a new style of life on the ground about 15 million years ago. What happened during the next 10 million years is still a mystery. We do know that at the end of that time, the first identifiable human ancestor had appeared.

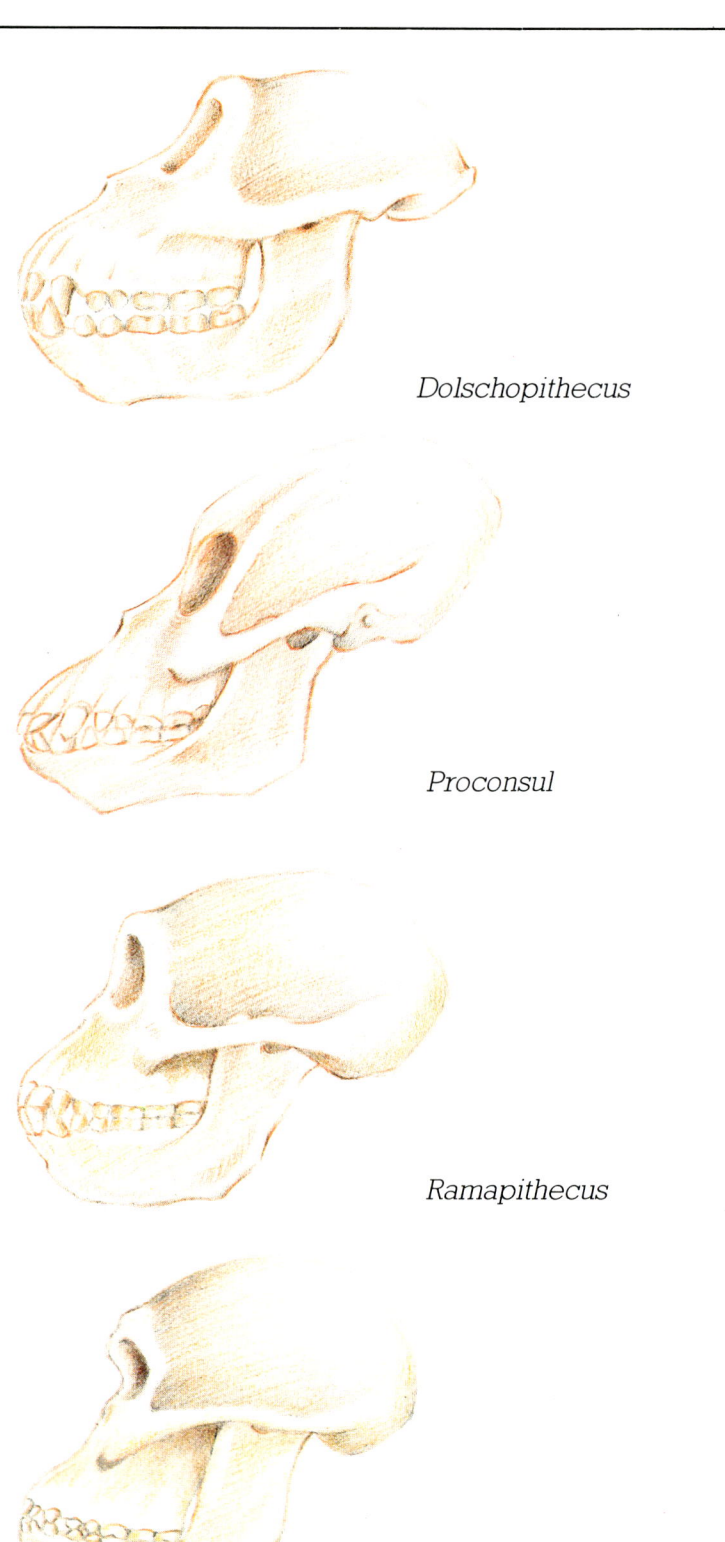

Dolschopithecus

Proconsul

Ramapithecus

Australopithecus africanus

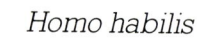

Homo habilis

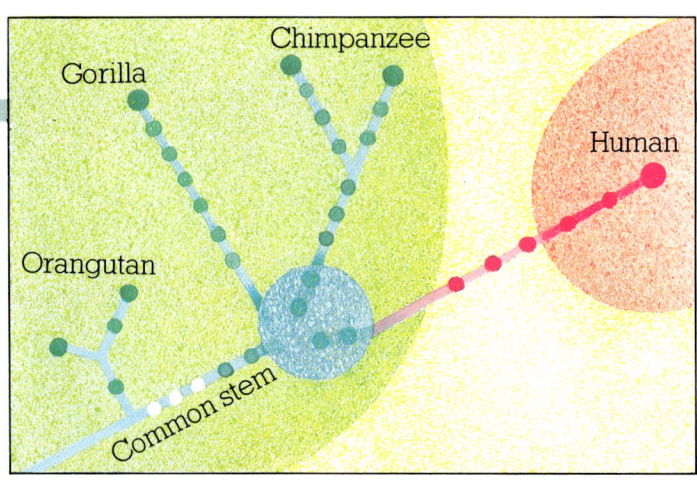

This diagram shows how the human family and the ape family began to grow apart.

The fossil skulls show how, in the journey from ape to human, the brain grew, the jaw shortened and the snout flattened into a nose.

A CRADLE IN AFRICA

In 1924, while digging for fossils in southern Africa, Professor Raymond Dart discovered some unusual, ape-like skulls and bones. He had never seen anything like them. After studying the bones, he decided that they could only be the remains of some of the earliest hominids. Other experts disagreed with him because the skulls were quite small, more like ape skulls. These experts believed that the ancestors of humans must have had larger brains than the apes and they argued that these skulls were too small to contain a larger, human brain.

The creature discovered by Professor Dart was named *Australopithecus*, which means 'ape of the south'. For many years nobody could explain what it was or where it might fit into the story of human evolution. Then, in 1959, the archaeologists Mary and Louis Leakey made a sensational discovery in the Olduvai Gorge in Tanzania, East Africa. Among the remains of some pebbles which had been chipped to make them into tools, they found a type of *Australopithecus* skull with a much larger brain than any previously found. They named this tool-making hominid, *Homo habilis*, which means 'handy man'. The find proved that apelike tool-makers had lived over 1,750,000 years ago.

This started a great fossil hunt throughout East Africa and, before long, remains of *Australopithecus* which were over 3 million years old were found alongside chipped pebbles. It began to look as if East Africa's Great Rift Valley, where so many of the fossils were found, might be the birthplace of modern humans.

One of the reasons for so many remains of these tool-using hominids being found in East Africa is that the Rift Valley, with its deep layers of sedimentary rock, is an excellent place for finding fossils. It may be possible that human beings evolved at around the same time in other places, but as yet no fossil evidence has been found which would prove this. The most likely explanation for the discovery of so many fossils of early hominids and their tools is that East Africa was indeed the starting point of the human race.

It is quite possible that something happened to the environment in this region between 2 and 4 million years ago which encouraged the development of groups of stone-using primates, or which forced the primates to start to use simple tools. The fact that the remains of early hominids have been found hardly anywhere else in the world, apart from in Java, seems to support this idea.

The most likely reason for four-footed primates beginning to walk upright is that the climate became drier. This caused the forests to shrink, forcing the primates to move to the ground to find food. Those who learned to stand upright and to use stones as tools would have been better protected from predators. They would have passed this skill on to their children.

The skull of an *Australopithecus*. Some of these creatures may have evolved into humans, but others appeared *after* the first human beings. *Australopithecus* has quite a small brain and so may be just another type of hominid and not the true ancestor of humans at all.

LUCY, A TEENAGE GIRL 3 MILLION YEARS OLD

Lucy was discovered in 1974 by anthropologist Donald C. Johanson during an international fossil-hunting expedition to Hadar in Ethiopia, East Africa. She is the most complete fossil skeleton of an ape-like hominid ever found and has an important place in the story of the origins of humans. She was given her name after the song, 'Lucy in the Sky with Diamonds', which was popular with the members of the expedition.

Lucy was probably eighteen years old when she died about 3 million years ago. At that time she was probably considered to be a very old lady. By looking at the many pieces of her skeleton, scientists worked out that she stood just over a metre high and weighed about thirty kilos. Her hip bone tells us she was female. Her pelvis, thigh and knee bones show that she walked upright. Her curved finger bones suggest that she occasionally took to the trees, perhaps to look for food or to find safety. So, although in some ways Lucy looked more like an ape, several things about her seem very human.

Lucy may have belonged to a group of ape-like creatures who were our direct ancestors. The problem is that other remains have been discovered in more or less the same area. These belong to hominids which looked much more human than Lucy although they lived at the same time as she did. These more human-looking hominids, called *Homo* meaning 'man' or 'being', obviously must belong to a quite different group from Lucy. So was it this group, Lucy's group or some other group which developed into humans? We probably will not know the answer until some older hominid fossils are found.

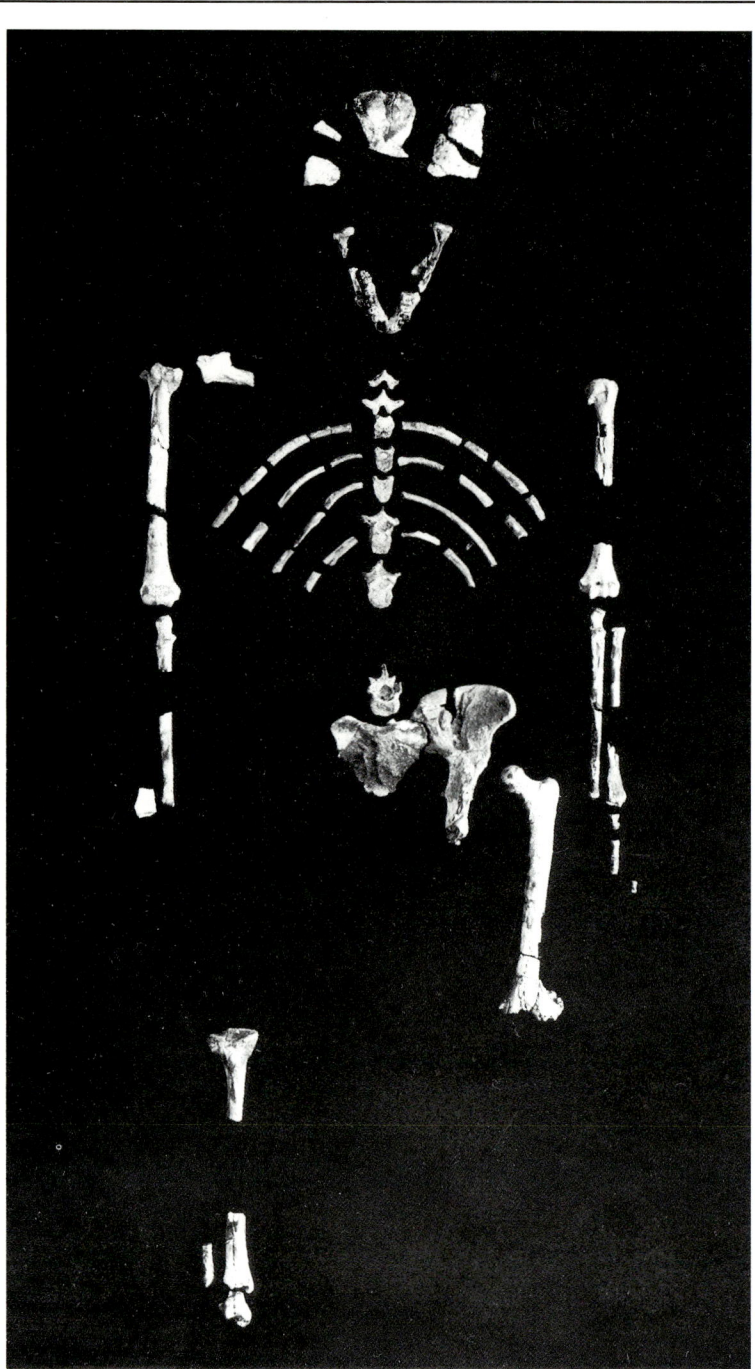

Lucy's bones were found in 1974. Using pieces of the jaw and teeth, scientists worked out what she must have looked like. Although they were similar in size to chimpanzees, females like Lucy gave birth more like humans do.

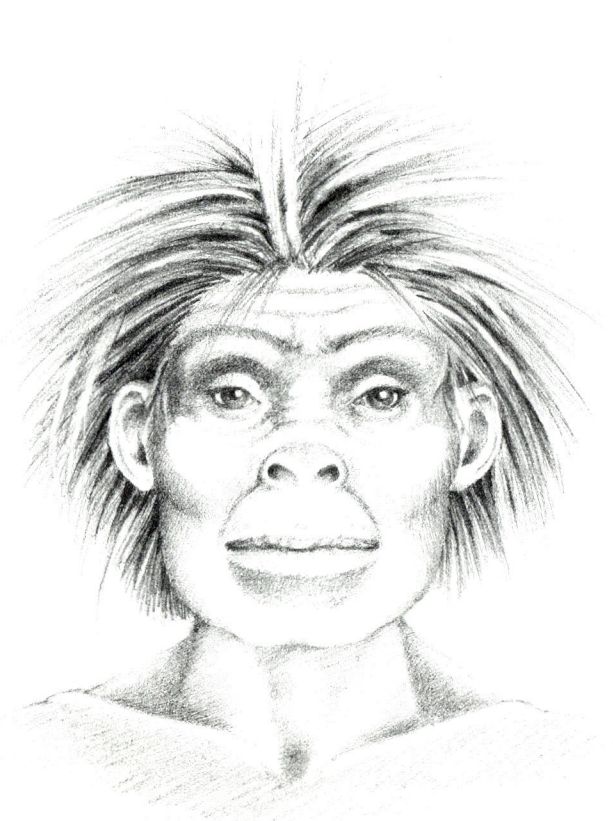

Lucy picking berries in
Ethiopia about 3 million
years ago.

THE FIRST TOOLS

Picture a bare plateau in Ethiopia, studded with a few twisted shrubs. The sun beats down on the sand and pebbles. This is Kada Gona, a site where the oldest known stone tools, some made 2,750,000 years ago, have been found.

These early tools are stones which have been chipped at one end to form a cutting edge. The tools look quite crude but we know that they were made deliberately and not by accident, because they have been methodically and carefully chipped from both sides. The tool-makers knew exactly what they wanted to achieve. They struck the left face of the stone, then the right face, until they had chipped enough off to make a cutting edge which was sharp enough for them to use. The smaller chips could be used as knives or scrapers, while the original stones could be used as hand-axes. These very simple but quite effective tools are the first examples of human technology.

Similar stone tools from a slightly later period have also been discovered at other sites in East Africa and in Morocco. Some of the stones have been fashioned very simply by being struck only once, but others show clear signs of having been chipped at least half a dozen times. These first stone tools come in all shapes and sizes, but they have one thing in common. All of them can be comfortably held in the hand.

What makes these tools important in the human story is that they are the first real proof of growing human intelligence. Chimpanzees use twigs to dig termites out of holes, and clumps of moss to soak up water for drinking, but no other animal except humans actually *makes* tools.

Some early humans in East Africa, over 2.5 million years ago. By this time people were not only making tools, but were also teaching their skills to others. The child watching the man will one day try to imitate him. Can the man give the child some advice? How can they communicate? It is now agreed that tool-makers must have had some kind of language, even if it was only made up of grunts and other simple sounds.

STONE TOOLS

Some of the very first stone tools. Chipped stones like these were used for 800,000 years before humans discovered how to make better hand-axes.

THE OMO VALLEY

The Omo Valley in East Africa is a treasure store of fossil remains. The valley, which is 1,000 metres deep, contains many layers of rock which hold the fossilised remains of hominids, early humans and their tools, animal remains and even pollen grains. The layers of rock are divided by layers of volcanic ash and lava. Since scientists are able to date the ash and lava, they can date the remains that lie above and below them. They can read the layers of fossil-bearing rock like the pages of a gigantic reference book. By looking at all the fossils together, scientists can build up a picture of how the hominids' development was affected by the surrounding climate, vegetation and animal life.

The fossil record shows that around 2 million years ago, australopithecines lived on open grasslands, where only a few trees grew. The land was filled with many different animals. These included giant warthogs, zebras, giraffes, baboons and even camels. These creatures were hunted by carnivores such as leopards, hyenas and the sabre-toothed tiger. Elephants, an elephant-like creature with downward-curving tusks called *Deinotherium*, and rhinoceroses wallowed in the water holes. The rivers teemed with crocodiles and hippopotamuses.

It seems that there was plenty of game for early hominids to hunt, but we cannot tell whether they did this or whether they just cut meat from animals which were already dead. However, it is obvious that the early hominids were slower than the game they may have hunted, and weaker than the predators of the time. So how could these small, near-human creatures have survived? We can guess that the only way they could have done so, and then thrived for about 2 million years, was by organising themselves into groups as a defence against predators, just as chimpanzees and baboons do today.

Tonnes of fossils have been found in the Omo Valley. From these fossils, scientists can guess what the valley looked like 2 million years ago.

THE OMO VALLEY TODAY
The sides of the valley are made up of rock layers. These provide a detailed record of the time when hominids were developing in this area.

PEOPLE START TO MOVE

Although the first hominids were born in the warm climate of East Africa, they didn't stay there. Between 2 million and 1 million years ago, hominids began to move to other areas. This 'conquest' of other lands was made possible because human evolution speeded up as tools were developed.

Many different types of these later human ancestors have been found. One is *Homo habilis*, the early tool-maker; another is *Homo erectus*, or 'upright being'. Whether these hominids were descended from *Australopithecus* or whether they are members of different groups of human ancestors is not yet clear.

Examples of *Homo erectus* have been found in many parts of the world, including Europe. The remains of other hominids, such as *Pithecanthropus* or 'ape-man', found in Java in 1891, and *Sinanthropus pekinensis* or 'Peking man', found in a large cave in China in 1927, are now believed to belong to the *Homo erectus* group.

These 'upright' people were very different from early hominids. Their skulls were thicker and they had large brow ridges above their eyes. Their brains were much larger and they walked upright all the time. They were taller, too; nearly as tall as modern people. This may be explained by the fact that they hunted in groups, so, unlike the earlier hominids who mostly gathered roots, nuts and berries, they had plenty of food.

Upright people, with their heavy bones and large brains, were well-equipped both physically and mentally to survive in colder areas, outside Africa. Some of them could make more advanced stone tools, such as hand-axes. They also knew how to build fires, though not necessarily how to light them. They may just have taken burning branches from forest fires and then kept a fire alight for as long as they could. Fire would have been useful not only to keep them warm, but also as protection from wild animals.

They probably moved around a good deal, leaving one area when plants and animals became scarce, and moving on to others where the food was plentiful. They may well have known how to build traps, such as pits to catch mammoths. They must have used the skins of the animals they killed to help keep out the cold.

Homo erectus hunters.

TOOLS, FIRE AND DEATH
THE ICE AGE

Roughly 2 million years ago the world became much colder. Glaciers began to form in a number of places, and these thick sheets of ice began to advance southwards. The Ice Age had begun.

Ice Ages have occurred several times in the history of the earth. They seem to happen every 200 million years or so, and may be caused by a change in the earth's angle of tilt, and variations in its path around the sun. The last Ice Age lasted until about 10,000 years ago, when the glaciers started to retreat.

The Ice Age actually consisted of about twenty short Ice Ages called 'glacials', which were followed by periods of warmer weather called 'interglacials'. During the glacials, huge areas of Europe, Asia and North America were covered with ice up to 3,000 metres deep. In order to survive, many animals, including humans, moved further south to find warmer weather, while others adapted to the cold. Some became smaller so they needed less food; others, such as the rhinoceros and the mammoth, grew thick hair.

The main effect of the Ice Age on the human story was that for about 200,000 years all trace of human life disappeared from Europe. Humans stayed in warmer regions to the south. They did not return until the climate became warmer and they discovered fire.

During the coldest periods of the Ice Age the Alps were almost entirely covered by ice. Only the highest mountain peaks thrust out through the glaciers.

The huge weight of the moving ice gouged smooth valleys in the softer rocks. When the ice retreated this valley in France became a lake which slowly filled with sediment. When the lake dried up the smooth sides were all that remained to show where the ice had passed.

HUNTING AND GATHERING

Our early ancestors lived by hunting wild animals and gathering fruits, seeds, berries and roots. Thanks to the discovery of sites which contain the remains of large numbers of slaughtered animals, we know a good deal about the hunting habits of the first people who came to Europe about 900,000 years ago.

Their diet included elephants, horses, hippopotamuses, stags and bison. The animals they killed were either quite old or very young, probably because the hunters found it much easier to attack the weaker animals, rather than to tackle fully-fit adult ones. Some types of *Homo erectus*, such as 'Peking man', killed large numbers of animals by driving whole herds over the edges of cliffs.

Although they did not know how to *make* fire, these early humans knew how to *use* fire. It is possible that they took burning branches from the edges of forest fires and used them to start their own fires which they kept burning for as long as possible. If this was the case, they may have cooked some of their meat, although it is likely that, for part of the time at any rate, they ate it raw.

We know less about the gathering done by these early people, because the remains of roots, tubers, fruits, nuts and seeds are impossible to find. We know the types of plants which grew in some areas at particular times by studying pollen fossils, but this does not tell us what was actually eaten. Just because dandelions were plentiful does not mean that people ate them!

Another way of finding out about prehistoric hunter-gatherers is to look at people today who still live in this way. Studies of this type have told us that the amount of gathering which goes on depends entirely on the natural resources of the area where the people live. Where vegetation is rich, gathering plants (and insects) can produce half the group's food supply. Where vegetation is scarce or non-existent, as in the northern polar regions where the Inuit live, hunting has to supply almost all the food.

Studying these modern hunter-gatherers shows that hunting and gathering is usually a communal activity, where everyone helps to find food for the whole group. If vegetation is scarce, men help with the gathering. If game is scarce, women help with the hunting, though they never seem to kill the animals themselves. It is probable that these people live in more or less the same way as our own ancestors did 500,000 years ago.

Humans have never lived on meat alone. Gathering fruits, nuts, berries, seeds, roots and tubers would have been a vital activity for early humans.

Humans, with their ability to use weapons and organise themselves into hunting groups, would have been more than a match for large animals such as hippopotamuses.

CAVES AND SHELTERS

Prehistoric people are often called 'cave men' or 'cave dwellers'. However, although we know by the remains which have been found that some groups of prehistoric people did live in caves, many more lived outside in the open air.

There were some advantages to be gained from living in caves. Inside a cave the temperature is a constant 10°C-12°C, which would have been welcome during cold winters. And it would have been easier to keep a fire going in the shelter of a cave.

However, not all areas have suitable caves. Most of the cave dwellers lived in limestone areas, where caves were formed by water eroding the rock. There may have been problems in staying in the same cave for a long time, since large amounts of hunting and gathering could lead to a shortage of food. Hunters and gatherers generally have to move around quite a lot, following the herds and looking for fresh supplies of roots, nuts and berries. For this reason, many of the best cave sites are near rivers which gave a plentiful supply of fish all year round.

These cave dwellers survived for over a million years, eating mainly raw meat and vegetables, and spending nights with only each other for warmth, clothed in skins and sheltered by their caves. Then at some stage they discovered the secret of making fire. Perhaps this happened while they were making stone tools, when sparks were produced by a flint striking a rock which contained iron ore.

Ancient cave dwellings provide a wealth of information for scientists studying prehistoric people. In the first place, the sites are more obvious and easier to find than sites in open country. Another advantage for archaeologists is that the traces of human habitation are usually well preserved in the soil of the cave floor. Secondly, the rocks, sand and clay of the cave floor provide valuable information about the climate. A very cold climate causes alternate freezing and thawing of the cave roof, which makes large blocks of stone break off and fall to the ground. Damp climate causes streams to rush through the cave carrying clay and pebbles with them. Stalactites and stalagmites form in mild climates. In dry climates the wind piles up fine particles. So, by looking at the layers on the floor, scientists can reconstruct the climate around a cave and date the remains they find at any particular depth.

Caves are mainly formed in limestone areas. The rocks are eaten away by water containing carbon dioxide. This forms a mild acid which dissolves the rock. Caves can extend far back into the rock.

Humans lived in caves between 400,000 and 700,000 years ago. They generally lived near the cave mouth, where they had both shelter and daylight.

The cave bear also liked to live in caves. Humans must have fought this ferocious creature to win the right to occupy a cave.

FIRE

Prehistoric people discovered the secret of making fire about 400,000 years ago. It was probably the most important advance in the human story. Fire provided people with warmth from the freezing winter weather through the long Ice Ages, a new weapon with which to scare off wild animals, and a means to cook food. However, the discovery of fire-making was much more than a major technological advance. It meant that humans had overcome an emotion shared by the entire animal kingdom – the fear of fire.

Fire brought many advantages, but it also held dangers. Early humans must have realised that they needed to control the fire they had made. To do this they surrounded the blazing wood with low stone walls, or else dug shallow pits in which to keep their fires. Not only did these first hearths stop the flames from spreading out of control and destroying the surrounding area, but they also sheltered the fire from the wind. This would have made the fire burn more efficiently, creating more heat and saving fuel.

Several types of hearth have been found. Some of the oldest have been discovered on the northern coast of France. Most of these early hearths are either round or square. Some have pebbles laid inside them on which the fire burned. The charcoal remains in these hearths show that oak was one of the most popular types of wood used in these early fires, though in some places broken bones also seem to have been used as fuel.

Many of the hearths which have been found are not in caves at all, but in open areas. Often they are found near the remains of the first huts. Among the oldest prehistoric houses found so far are two which were discovered in East Germany. They were built over 300,000 years ago.

Prehistoric houses were generally either round or oval. They were usually very small, only about three metres by four metres, with low stone walls and wooden posts to support the roofs. Some of them had floors which were paved with pebbles.

The mastery of fire seems to have happened at about the time that humans began to build homes for themselves. It is almost as if one could not have happened without the other. It is as if, even in those distant days, hearth and home had to be created together.

The discovery of fire must have changed
human behaviour. Early humans would
have gathered round the fireside to share
ideas, conversation and dreams. Perhaps
this led to the development of religion.
On the left you can see the remains of one
of the earliest hearths.

STONE-CUTTING

As we have seen, the first tools for cutting were fashioned by chipping small stones. Gradually, over hundreds of thousands of years, prehistoric people found ways of making better tools.

The first of these new, improved tools was made in East Africa about 1,500,000 years ago. It was a hand-axe, shaped on both sides. This type of hand-axe is called a biface, because it has two faces. The biface axe was made out of flint, which is an ideal material for making stone tools because, when struck correctly, it flakes easily, leaving a sharp edge. A skilful stone-cutter could strike the flint many times to fashion a well-designed and much more useful tool. However, these improved tools were not easy to make and so, for many thousands of years, roughly-cut stone tools of the older type were used in larger numbers than the new flint axe.

About 500,000 years ago, another new stone-working skill developed. The stone-cutters gradually realised that certain flint stones, if prepared and struck in the correct way, could produce not just one, but many useful tools. To do this the worker prepared a core by chipping all round the flint. An accurate final blow produced a stone blade. Each single piece, or 'flake', produced like this was a finished tool. Some were thin, razor-sharp slivers which could be used as knives or arrowheads.

It is obvious that the workers who made these advanced stone tools had to prepare and plan what they did in advance, rather than simply try to produce tools by trial and error. This shows an enormous advance in human intelligence, although the development of the skill did not happen overnight.

Tool-makers chipping flint stones.

THE BIFACE AXE

These stones were deliberately worked to produce an almond-shaped hand-axe. The rounded end was held in the hand, and the other end had either a point or a cutting edge. The hand-axe lasted over a million years – longer than any other tool.

Montières-Etouvy
(Somme)enCorbin
Basse terrasse Sept.1912
117

Montières-Etouvy
(Somme)esrnière Corbin
Nucleus Levalloisien
Basse terrasse Sept.1912
+16 m.
108

TOOTH AND CLAW

Early books on prehistoric life usually describe our ancestors as hairy, brutish people dressed in untidy skins and armed with clumsy weapons, constantly fighting with cave bears, hairy mammoths and giant lions. In fact, our distant ancestors were well adapted to surviving in their time and had developed good weapons as well as efficient hunting methods.

It is true that some of the animals of the time were bigger and stronger than those of today. There was a prehistoric cave lion which was larger than a present-day lion. There was an elephant called *meridionalis* which stood four metres high at the shoulders, nearly a metre higher than a modern elephant. Another giant was the *Megaloceros*, a huge deer whose antlers were double the size of those of stags today. There was a very large wild ox, called the aurochs, which stood over two metres high at the shoulders. On the other hand, many prehistoric animals were actually smaller than their descendants. The bears, for example, were no larger than a present-day grizzly and the mammoth was actually smaller than the modern elephant.

There were also many smaller prehistoric animals which were very fierce, such as the wolf. However the hyenas, foxes, deer, and the wide variety of birds were almost identical to those we know today. Many of these animals no longer live in Europe. Some have been wiped out by humans, others simply starved to death, unable to migrate freely from north to south to find food when their habitat no longer supported them because of the high mountain barrier which lies across Europe. In America, where the mountains run north to south, the animals could migrate freely, moving towards warmer areas which contained more food. This allowed a wider variety of animal life to survive there.

In some places, huge amounts of animal remains have been found, along with stone and bone implements, wooden stakes and spears. These show that, at certain times, several groups of people must have gathered and joined together for large-scale hunts. Humans, with their greater intelligence, were able to organise themselves, survive and live off the hostile environment which surrounded them. Brainpower almost always proved itself to be superior to the strength and ferocity of the wild animals of the prehistoric world.

The fossil remains of horses are quite common in prehistoric sites. One type of horse that resembles its prehistoric ancestors has survived – the little Przewalski horse which can still be found in central Asia.

The *Megaloceros* was the largest of several types of deer in prehistoric times. Its antlers were 4m across.

The woolly rhinoceros was specially adapted to survive the cold of the Ice Age.

An aurochs and a reindeer. They must have been very important to prehistoric people, as they are often shown in cave paintings.

THE DISCOVERY OF DEATH

Between 100,000 and 50,000 years ago, a very important new idea grew in the human mind. Excavations of the sites of the period show that certain groups of people, particularly the Neanderthals, were beginning to bury their dead. Some of the graves which have been discovered by archaeologists contain not only complete skeletons, but also many different types of objects which had obviously been placed deliberately beside the body.

Many of the graves were dug in the floors of the caves in which the Neanderthals lived. Some of the bodies were buried singly, others were buried in groups. Many of them had their legs drawn up to their chests, and sometimes, where several graves have been found, the bodies in them all pointed in the same direction. All this indicates that these prehistoric people gave considerable thought to the burials. The fact that several bodies have been found in the same place has led some scientists to believe that certain areas may have been put aside as special graveyards, although there is not really enough evidence to prove this.

The objects buried alongside the bodies in these prehistoric graves are generally tools, such as reindeer-antler picks and flint hand-axes. Some animal bones have also been found, which indicates that food was buried with the body. The care that the prehistoric people took in burying their dead seems to show that those who did the burying had some idea there might be a life after death. The tools and food which they buried with the bodies would be needed by the dead to lead their second life, which the Neanderthals must have thought was going to be very like their first life on earth.

A double Neanderthal grave. The bodies are those of an old woman and a teenager. You can see how their legs have been drawn up towards their chests. Another grave found in Czechoslovakia contained twenty bodies, all of them children or babies.

A GRAVE IN FRANCE

The skeletons of two adults and five children were found in this grave in the Dordogne region of France. They were buried with three tools which all pointed in the same direction.

There are no traces of any graves before the Neanderthal period, so it is assumed that these people were the first to bury their dead. Many of the bodies are those of children, which is quite remarkable as children's bones are more fragile and do not last as long as those of adults.

THE NEANDERTHALS

Neanderthals lived between 125,000 and 30,000 years ago in parts of Europe and the Near East. They were shorter and more thick-set than modern people. They had broad faces, chinless jaws, low foreheads, heavy brow ridges and flattened noses. The average size of a Neanderthal's brain was at least as large as, if not larger than, that of a modern person. Neanderthals were the first examples of *Homo sapiens*, or 'knowing being'.

The fact that Neanderthals buried their dead has meant that more of their remains have been found than the remains of any hominids that lived before them.

Neanderthals made flint tools and were probably very intelligent. Their tough bodies were well adapted for living in the last of the Ice Ages. For some reason which is not yet understood, the Neanderthals mysteriously died out around 30,000 years ago.

When the Neanderthals became extinct, another type of human had already been established for over 20,000 years. This was a form of *Homo sapiens sapiens*, or 'modern people'. They were called *Cro-Magnons*, after the place where they were found in France. Some have suggested that the Cro-Magnons may have killed off all the Neanderthals, but there is no evidence for this. These Cro-Magnons were hunter-gatherers for about 40,000 years. Then, about 9,000 years ago, they made another great leap forward in the human story by inventing farming. Somehow they discovered the secret of taming certain animals such as sheep, goats, pigs and cattle. To begin with, they drove their herds with them. Many nomadic people still do this.

However, a much more important discovery was that they learned how to grow crops. They might have done this by noticing that certain sorts of food plants always grew in the same places, year after year. Then they discovered that they could plant seeds which grew the following year. Soon they were experimenting with all kinds of different plants. Before long, these first farmers began to live near their new fields of crops to guard them from animals or other humans. They abandoned their nomadic life and began to settle down. It was not long afterwards that the first civilisations appeared.

This is where the opening chapters of the human story end. It is an incredible adventure which has lasted about 4 million years. During this period, humans evolved from ape-like creatures called *Australopithecus* to *Homo habilis, Homo erectus, Homo sapiens* and finally *Homo sapiens sapiens*, or modern people. The adventure still continues.

A typical Neanderthal skull.

Neanderthals were the first form of *Homo sapiens*. They were also the first humans to bury their dead.

Discovering a site

Prehistoric sites are sometimes discovered by accident. There are many examples of how people have more or less stumbled across ancient remains. One of the best-known examples of this was the discovery of the famous Lascaux caves, in France. These contain the most magnificent prehistoric wall paintings which have yet been found anywhere in the world. They were accidentally discovered by young boys who were exploring a hillside. However, many prehistoric sites lie in more open areas, hidden under many tonnes of earth. They are more often found when land is being dug up for road construction, during major building projects or as a result of planned excavations of a suspected archaeological site.

If an important site is discovered during a major building project, the construction company will usually stop work for a while to allow archaeologists to investigate the ancient remains. Under these circumstances the archaeologists have to race against time to complete a hurried dig, before the evidence is lost or covered over. Digs done under these circumstances are called rescue archaeology.

An archaeologist uncovering the remains of a fossilised elephant on one of the sites in the Omo Valley. Fossil bones are often very fragile so they are encased in plaster or soaked in resin to allow them to be moved safely. They are glued together and examined in a laboratory.

Rescue archaeology

Any large-scale building or road construction scheme will involve years of planning, hundreds of workers and millions of pounds. It is most unlikely that anyone will be able to stop it for long, even if a valuable archaeological site is discovered. Any excavations done on sites discovered in this way will have to be carried out very quickly before work is resumed and the site is destroyed. Under these circumstances the policy in most European countries is to organise rescue excavations.

Sometimes rescue excavations are planned in advance. Archaeological organisations are constantly notified of any building plans, and archaeologists tell the authorities what might be found under a proposed building development. The archaeologists then ask for some time to do excavations before the building actually begins. Once they have done everything they can in the time available, the builders move in and start their work. After this, the site is probably lost to the archaeologists for ever. It is only very rarely that a site is important enough for the building works to be altered to preserve the remains, although this has happened in York and London.

As time is always short, the archaeologists often make advance surveys of likely sites to find out as much as they can about the area. This saves them wasting precious hours during the dig itself. Sometimes they do this by taking photographs from the air. Details which cannot be seen on the ground will show up quite clearly in aerial photographs, especially in the early morning or evening, when the shadows are long.

Other valuable information about a site can be gathered by measuring variations in the electrical resistance or the magnetism in the soil. In towns and cities, where sites are at greatest risk, archaeologists often prepare maps in advance, just in case a site might be developed. Maps like this have already been drawn up for several major European cities, including London.

Of course, where a site is in the open countryside, there is usually plenty of time for a detailed excavation, so the archaeologists do not have to race against time in the same way. Often sites are in remote places, as in the Omo Valley in East Africa, for instance, where most of the oldest known tools and the remains of the earliest human beings have been found. In cases like this, archaeologists often mount major international expeditions which visit and work at the site for months or even years.

Archaeological finds

During the nineteenth century, the first archaeologists and prehistorians used teams of labourers with picks and shovels to do the digging for them. Their main aim was to unearth the most spectacular finds they could. Their work was done very quickly and unscientifically. What they did was often little better than looting and caused terrible damage to many sites. We may never know how much information about the past has been lost through bad archaeology.

Modern archaeologists conducting a dig are much more careful and scientific in their approach. They want to extract as much information as they can from the site. In order to achieve this, every single find must be carefully logged, drawn, photographed, and its position recorded. Even the smallest fragments are collected. It is no longer thought good enough to pick up a flint tool. The modern prehistorian also collects the smallest flakes which were chipped off the tool when it was made. The same is true of bones, which are often found in pieces. Some of these fragments are too tiny to be seen with the naked eye, and must be collected by sifting the soil.

The soil itself has to be examined minutely. It may contain ash and charcoal. Patches may have been coloured by fire. These patches are also recovered by sifting or exposed by careful brushing, and their positions are carefully mapped. So a modern dig is much more thorough, and everything, including the actual soil, can be part of the find.

It is also thought vital to observe and record the relationships between all the different finds. If two pieces were once joined – for example, two fragments of flint found a metre apart, which turn out to fit together – the relationship between them is as important as the objects themselves. Their position may show where a tool was made, as well as whether it was a success or whether it was thrown away in disgust.

Once the findings have been recorded, the archaeologist may then spend years analysing the finds. The scientists study, piece together and test discoveries. This can only be done if the original finds were uncovered very carefully.

A series of footprints discovered in Tanzania, East Africa. Two australopithecines walked here 3.7 million years ago. They are the oldest human footprints yet discovered. Plastic moulds of the footprints can reveal an enormous amount about the hominids who made them, provided these fragile marks have not been damaged by more modern feet!

One of the earliest sites of human habitation, at Melka Kunture in Ethiopia, East Africa. Among the finds were paving stones and an earth platform which were about 1.5 million years old.

In general, the older the site, the more difficult it will be for the archaeologist to work out what was there originally. This site proves that Homo habilis or early Homo erectus were able to organise their lives. The earth platform may have been a sleeping or living area. Some of the piles of stones may have been some kind of wall – though that does not necessarily mean that there was a roof.

SURVIVORS OF THE PREHISTORIC AGE

In certain remote parts of the world, there are people living today who use only stone and wooden tools. One is a tribe of farmers who live in the jungles of New Guinea. Until recently they had no contact with the outside world and no knowledge of metal. Some bushmen in the southern African desert still live the free life of their hunting ancestors. In South America many Amazon Indians still follow a Stone Age way of life.

Many of these ancient cultures have been destroyed by contact with western 'civilisation'. Some groups, such as the North American Indians, have been systematically driven from their lands and confined to reservations. Although these people are often described as 'primitive', scientists now recognise that they are in fact organised into well-developed societies which are in tune with their environment.

An Aborigine man making fire by rubbing sticks together. This method was used by the earliest people.

A long history

Other groups have managed to survive and preserve their culture in spite of the pressures of twentieth-century civilisation. The Pygmies of the African rain forests nearly lost their culture as they became servants to the farming peoples who lived around them. However, before lasting damage could be done, many of them returned to their forest life. Here they revived their unusual hunting skills. These included hunting elephants with long nets. Once snared, the trapped animal was finished off by a single hunter armed with only a spear.

Some groups, such as the Australian Aborigines, have taken active steps to protect their culture. They have been badly treated since the seventeeth century, but they have not died out, although, over the years, many of their tribal lands have been given to mining companies who have paid them nothing in return. Recently they have been given back some of their former lands. Since then, the Aborigines have become fiercely protective of any sites which have significance for them. They have restricted access to areas which are sacred to them, where there are rock paintings and burial sites. The Aborigines make strict distinctions between male and female activities, so they have banned female scientists altogether. Even male scientists have difficulty in getting official permission to visit sacred areas or to go to places where they can study examples of Aboriginal art.

Unfortunately the restoration of the old lands has come too late for hundreds of Aboriginal rock paintings and engravings. Although these were cared for and regularly restored for thousands of years, during the last century, while Aborigines were unable to visit the sites, they have begun to decay and even to disappear. Much has therefore been lost already by the selfishness of the early European settlers.

However, the Aborigines have managed to keep many of their old customs going. In 1984, for instance, a number of tribes travelled 1,500 kilometres in a convoy of trucks to take part in the ceremony of 'The Two Dream Sisters', which had not been performed for over a hundred years.

The rich history, the powerful family relationships, the beliefs and the daily

Bushmen of the Kalahari Desert in South Africa gather food and hunt just as their ancestors did thousands of years ago.

activities of these ancient peoples can provide much new information to scientists who are studying the ancient Stone Age. But although the stone tools, implements and remains which have been found can tell us something of the lives of prehistoric people, the hard flint cannot say much about the thoughts and feelings of their makers. It is largely through studies of these modern Stone Age groups that scientists can begin to build up a more complete picture of prehistoric life.

The last of the Alakalufs

Sadly, many of these early peoples have long since vanished. Their societies were too fragile to survive contact with our civilisation. History is littered with examples of tribes and even empires which were destroyed by contact with the European explorers of the fifteenth and sixteenth centuries, and by the imperial expansions of the nineteenth century. The Aztec Empire of Mexico and the Inca Empire of Peru are two such civilisations which disappeared, leaving behind their stone cities as the only monuments to their passing.

Stone Age societies which have been found more recently are not deliberately destroyed by their discoverers, but begin to disintegrate under the pressures of twentieth-century life. One example of such a society was the Alakaluf Indians of Tierra del Fuego, an island off the tip of South America. Since the 1930s the young members of the tribe have gradually left, preferring to live in Chile rather than to follow the old ways of the tribe.

The Alakalufs lived in huts made from pole frames bound together with rushes and covered with sealskins. The walls were made of bark, and any gaps were plugged with grass and leaves. Branches were piled on either side of the doorway to keep out draughts. The Alakalufs slept on leaves and dried grass, using deerskins as covers.

They wore capes made from sealskin or other smaller skins such as otter, sewn together with whale sinew. The men wore loincloths. The women wore shell necklaces, and the men wore headdresses, bracelets and neckpieces made from feathers. The men also wore hats made from seagulls' wings. They used bows and arrows, slings, harpoons and nooses to hunt.

An anthropologist who visited the tribe in the 1950s found that they had dropped many of their customs, in particular the painting of their bodies. They still sang sometimes and played a few games, but most of the time they sat in silence. They seemed to know that they had nearly reached their end.

Eskimos call themselves the Inuit, which means 'human beings'. Some of them are descendants of people who migrated across the Bering Strait around 8,000 years ago. At their settlements, archaeologists have dug up fine stone blades similar to some found in Siberia. This shows that contact did exist between Asia and America.

THE MYSTERY OF THE FIRST AMERICANS

A long migration

For a long time it was thought that the first Americans must have arrived on the continent about 12,000 years ago. The main reason for this was that most of the remains which have been found date from that period. These include some fine tools, hunting weapons and the bones of animals killed by early hunters.

However, this theory poses a major problem. The descendants of the Indians who came to Alaska from Asia must have spread out into the interior and moved slowly down towards Central and South America. However, sites that are 10,000 years old have been found throughout the entire length of North and South America. This would mean, therefore, that the whole continent from Alaska, across the Great Plains, round the Gulf of Mexico, through Central America, across the Amazon jungle and down to Tierra del Fuego was populated in no more than 2,000 years. This would have been quite impossible.

This idea has changed recently. Thanks to new archaeological discoveries, it is now believed that the first Americans must have arrived much earlier than had been thought before.

It seems likely that the first Americans arrived in Alaska on foot during the Ice Age. They were probably Indians living on the continent of Asia, who were following the herds of large mammals they hunted. Quite by accident, they found themselves in Alaska.

At this time, while the North and South Poles were surrounded by enormous sheets of ice, the sea level had dropped by 120 metres, so the 76-kilometre-wide Bering Strait, which separates Asia from America, was a land bridge between the two continents. Reaching Alaska at that time would have been a very simple matter.

Prehistorians are certain that the first Americans walked in from the northwest, rather than by crossing the Arctic ice from Russia or hopping from island to island across the Pacific Ocean tens of thousands of years before boats had been invented! However, while they are quite sure how they came, the scientists are not at all sure *when* the first inhabitants of America arrived.

One of the reasons for believing this is that sites have been discovered in Mexico which were inhabited by humans over 27,000 years ago. These are mainly hunting grounds, where the remains of large herbivores have been found alongside simple stone and bone tools.

Even earlier sites have been discovered in parts of South America. Tools estimated to be 33,000 years old have been found in Chile. In north-west Brazil an excavation team has found the remains of a shelter which is 32,000 years old. There may be still older remains below this site.

These finds show that parts of the American continent were inhabited about 30,000 years ago. It seems logical that if South America *was* inhabited around 30,000 years ago, then North America must have been populated a good deal earlier.

The Yukon site

It must have taken many thousands of years for people to spread down from the Bering Straits to Patagonia at the tip of South America. However, very little evidence has been found which *proves*

There are only a few thousand Jivaro Indians now. They are one of the tribes living in the forests in the foothills of the Andes mountains in Peru. Like most of the Amazon Indians, they have lived for centuries by hunting, fishing and gathering. They also farm plots of land which they leave when the goodness of the soil is exhausted. Sometimes they live in clans, but more often they live in small families. The Jivaros are among the most warlike people in the world. They are constantly at war with other members of their tribe. They seem to fight simply because they enjoy it.

that North America was settled before the South. The only clues that point to this are provided by a site in the Yukon in north-western Canada. Bones which are probably over 40,000 years old, which were worked by humans and which could have been used as tools, have been found on the banks of the Old Crow river. Huge amounts of split animal bones, which may have been cracked by human hunters as long as 150,000 years ago, have also been found there.

This much earlier date is much more promising. It could be the evidence which archaeologists need to show when the great migration of early tribes began. The fact that it started much earlier than scientists had previously thought is also interesting, because a slow spread of small groups of humans would account for the great variety of people and languages which later appeared in America. It is estimated, for instance, that there were 2,200 spoken languages on the American continents before the Europeans arrived.

The American: a recent immigrant?

It seems likely that the first Americans crossed the Bering Strait about 150,000 years ago. However, the first people in Africa, Europe and Asia appeared much earlier than this. A site which might be 1.5 million years old has recently been discovered in eastern Siberia, not far from the Bering Strait. Has this some connection with the first Americans? What prehistorians want to find now are the actual remains of early American humans. However, not so much as a single jaw or finger bone of the correct date has yet been found. With only tools and animal bones of the correct date to help us, we still have no idea of what the first Americans looked like.

CONTINENTAL DRIFT

One of the most important clues to the history of the earth was only discovered recently, in 1960. Before then, geologists could describe how the map of the world had changed, but they could not explain how the continents had formed and then drifted apart.

The theory of continental drift was first proposed early in this century by an Austrian geologist, Alfred Wegener. He drew attention to the geological similarities between separate continents, and pointed out that some of their edges seemed to match each other like pieces of a jigsaw puzzle.

Wegener suggested that there had once been one vast super-continent made up of South America, Africa, Madagascar, Antarctica, India and Australia, which later broke into pieces. These pieces then drifted slowly into their present positions.

The great rift

Until the 1960s, most scientists did not believe Wegener's theory. However, studies of the ocean depths were to prove them right. Surveys of ocean floors led to the discovery that all over the world the sea bottom is crossed by deep rifts, lying between parallel ridges. In the Atlantic, one great rift winds from north to south, practically midway between the Old World and the New World. The rift continues southward, past Africa, then crosses the Indian Ocean.

The rocks forming this rift are volcanic. In fact, the rift is shaken by regular volcanic eruptions. The lava has been spewing up through the faults in the crust of the earth for millions of years. As the molten lava oozes through the cracks in the ocean floor it is cooled by the sea and forms new ocean crust. As a result, the ocean floor has been expanding, pushing the continents apart. In general the top of the Mid-Atlantic Ridge lies between 2,000 and 3,000 metres below the surface, but in some places the ridge has risen out of the ocean and formed islands such as the Azores.

It has now been established that the Atlantic began to expand around 180 million years ago and is still growing at the rate of a few centimetres per year. This continual movement of the ocean floor is gradually pushing Africa and America even further apart.

Drifting continents

There are other oceanic rifts, east of Japan and west of South America. Here the oceanic crust produced thousands of kilometres away has pushed its way under the lighter continental crust. The enormous friction produced as one crust slides under the other causes earthquakes. As the rock plunges back into the magma, it provides fresh fuel for the volcanoes which are formed along the edge of the rift.

The island chain which includes Japan and the immense mountain chain of the Andes was produced by the swallowing up of the oceanic crust, a process called subduction.

The earth's crust is divided into a number of large plates. The study of the movement of these plates is called 'plate tectonics'. In some places the plates slide alongside each other, causing earthquakes. In other places the plates are moving apart, creating volcanoes, or colliding, creating earthquakes and volcanoes.

This satellite photograph shows the Great Lakes area of the East African Great Rift Valley. Not far from Lake Nation (marked with a yellow box) is the Olduvai site, the cradle of the human race. The Rift Valley is a split in the African plate. However, unlike the Red Sea rift, this split is no longer widening.

Over 120 million years ago, where the Himalayan mountains now rise, a huge ocean lapped the shores of two continents. Over hundreds of thousands of years the plates which carried these continents moved together. The enormous pressure pushed the ocean floor upwards to form the Himalayan mountain chain. This is why fossils are found at altitudes of 6,000 metres. They are the remains of sea creatures who once lived on an ocean floor which has been raised up by the movements of plates.

The movement of these plates still continues. India started pushing into Asia about 55 million years ago and has been moving at a rate of five centimetres per year ever since.

Future collisions

Further collisions will happen in the future. The African plate is moving away from America and is rotating steadily towards Europe. Eventually this movement will close up the eastern Mediterranean altogether. This will probably happen in about 14 million years time, a relatively quick process in geological terms.

The smaller plates are often caught up in the movements of the larger ones. The plate on which Italy lies was pushed by other plates into Europe to create the Alps. The plate on which Spain lies has been pushed in several directions until, about 100 million years ago, it rubbed against Europe and created the Pyrenees. While the eastern Mediterranean is closing, the Red Sea is slowly opening up. If the movement continues in the same way for about 200 million years, the Red Sea will become an ocean. As Arabia and Asia come into contact, the earthquakes which have already started there could continue for thousands of years to come.

These maps show the movement of the continental plates from the start of the Palaeozoic era to the beginning of the Tertiary period. One enormous supercontinent (called Pangaea) can be seen forming towards the end of the Palaeozoic era 300 million years ago.

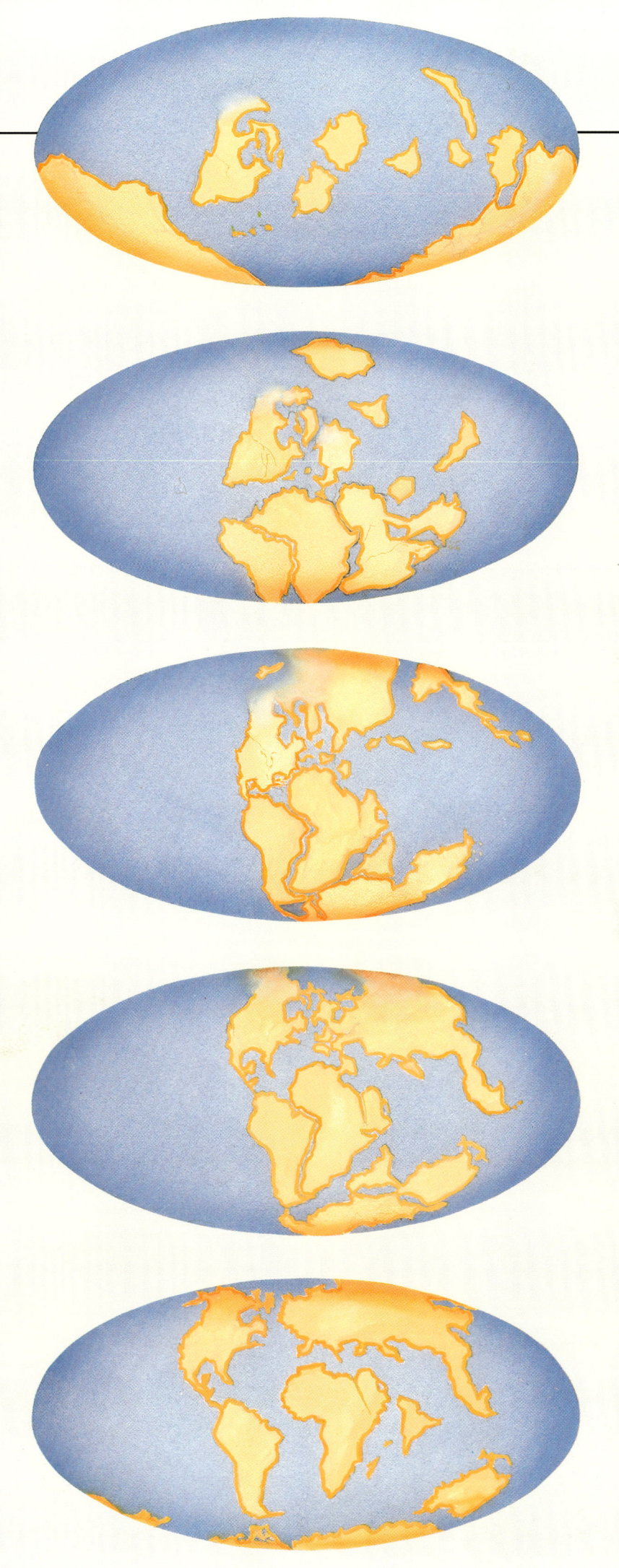

THE END OF THE UNIVERSE

The stars are dying. Scientists calculate that galaxies – perhaps even the universe – will have an end. What will become of our universe, born 15 billion years ago in a 'big bang'?

We know of stars that have died or are in the process of dying. One of these is Sirius B. This is the companion star of the giant Sirius, and lies about eleven light years away from us. As Sirius B dies it is slowly cooling and has now become very dense. Because it looks small and white, it is called a White Dwarf.

Other dying stars are even smaller and denser than White Dwarfs. These are called neutron stars. Some neutron stars give out short bursts or pulses of radio waves as they spin around in their death throes. They are called pulsars.

However, not all dying stars shrink. Large stars end their lives in a gigantic explosion called a supernova.

The death of the Sun

How a star dies depends mainly on its size. Our sun is a relatively small star, 1,390,000 kilometres in diameter. It will carry on shining as it is now for another 5 billion years or more. However, there will eventually come a time when it has burned up all its hydrogen. Then its core will contract, its temperature will rise to about 56 million°C and its exterior will expand to 100 times its present size and 500 times its present brightness. The sun's rays will blaze down, increasing the temperature on the earth to about 1,500°C! For about 250 million years, the sun will be a red giant. Then there will be a violent explosion which will cause all the helium on the sun to fuse together. This process will take several hundred million years.

Finally, there will be a very unstable and very bright phase, during which the sun will eject most of its mass, leaving only a hot, shining core which will start to contract. Eventually the sun will turn into a White Dwarf. Its volume will be roughly the same as the earth's, but it will be fantastically dense. The sun will then slowly cool and turn gradually into a Black Dwarf, which it will remain for billions of years.

Stars which are much larger than the sun behave in a different way. At the end of their lives they explode, throwing out matter which scatters through space to provide material for new stars. These exploding stars are called supernovas. After the explosion, only the centre of the star is left. This centre, which is even denser than a White Dwarf, is called a neutron star. A neutron star with the same mass as the sun measures only about twenty-four kilometres in diameter.

The force of gravity acting on one of these small but extremely dense neutron stars is extremely powerful. Scientists now believe that neutron stars continue to contract, until, eventually, they are only six kilometres across. At this point the force of gravity on the surface of the star becomes so great that nothing, not even light, can escape from it. The star has become a black hole.

Since light cannot escape from black holes, they are invisible. Although scientists believed as long as 200 years ago that they did exist, they were not able to prove that they did. For many years scientists tried to locate black holes by observing the effect of their gravitational pull on other objects. During the 1970s,

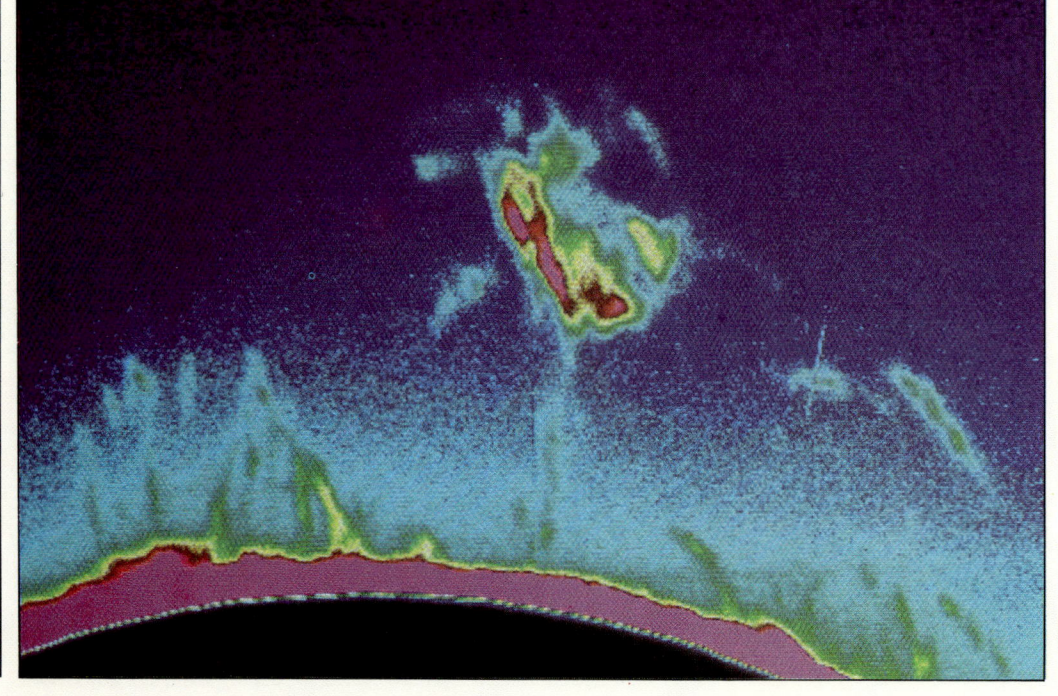

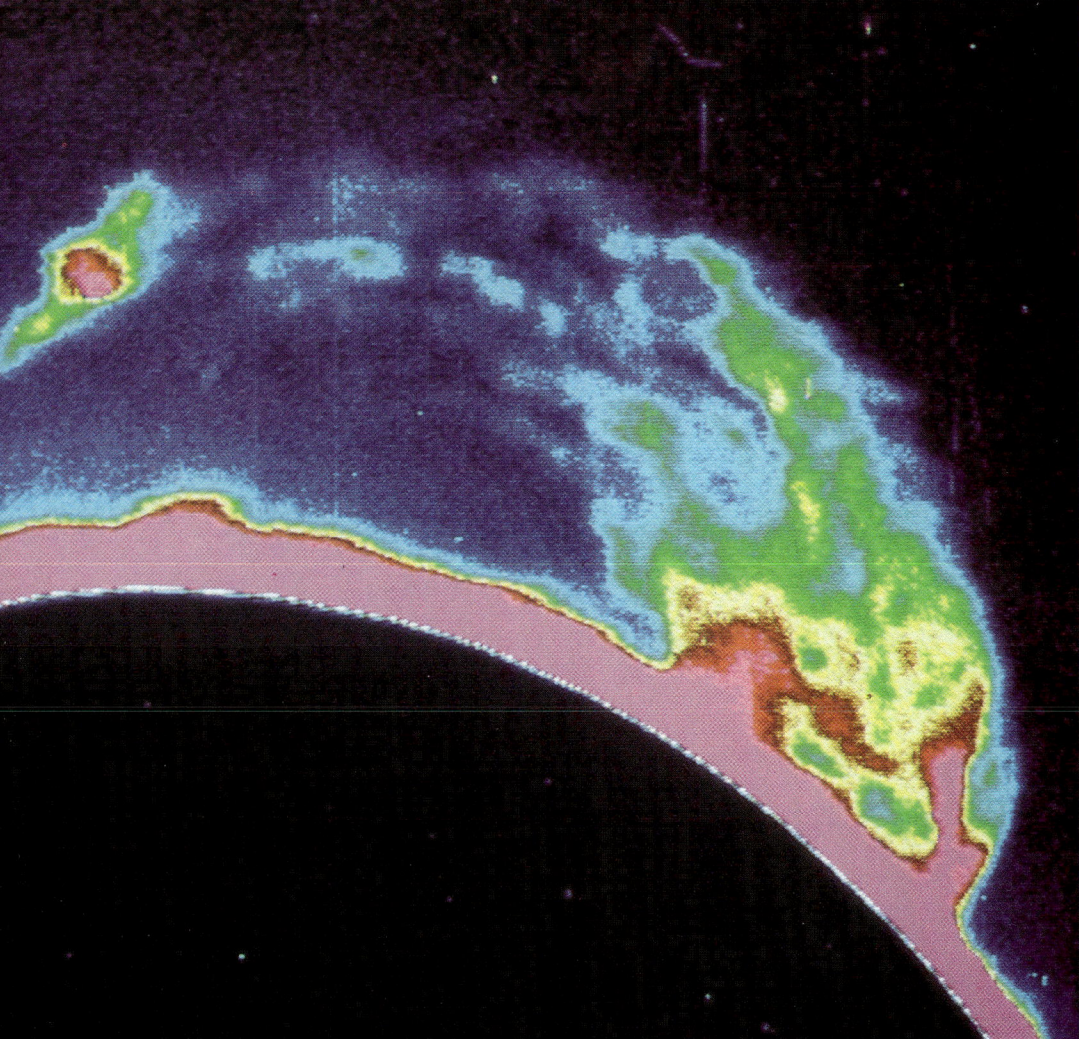

neutron stars; black holes; some small, cold asteroids; and a little dust.

Another thousand billion years after that, most of the stars, though dead, will have escaped from the galaxy as a result of collisions, and the rest will have gathered together into a single mass of dead stars which will collapse into a colossal black hole. Eventually, thousands of billions of years later, other dead galaxies will fall into this black hole, creating a supergalactic black hole, 300 billion kilometres in diameter.

Some people think that billions of billions of years after that, even the black holes will somehow fade away, leaving a universe full of rocks, expanding and cooling. It would be like the big bang which began the universe happening in reverse.

some astronomers discovered a star that seemed to rotate around an invisible object in the constellation Cygnus. They believed that this must be a black hole. Other possible black holes have been located in the centre of the Milky Way and in the galaxy called the Large Magellanic Cloud.

Then, in the early 1980s, a different method of locating black holes was used. Scientists realised that the powerful gravity of black holes attracted gas and dust from nearby stars. Just as a meteor falling through the earth's atmosphere will heat up, so these objects also give off heat. Instruments mounted in spacecraft were able to measure this heat and have recently located a number of black holes in our own solar system.

The end of the end

This raises the question of what will happen after our sun dies. What will happen when all the material available to make new stars has disappeared, and when the galaxy contains nothing but dead stars?

Eventually there will come a time, probably in about 1,000 million years, when our galaxy will contain practically nothing but dead bodies. All that remains will be Black Dwarfs; White Dwarfs;

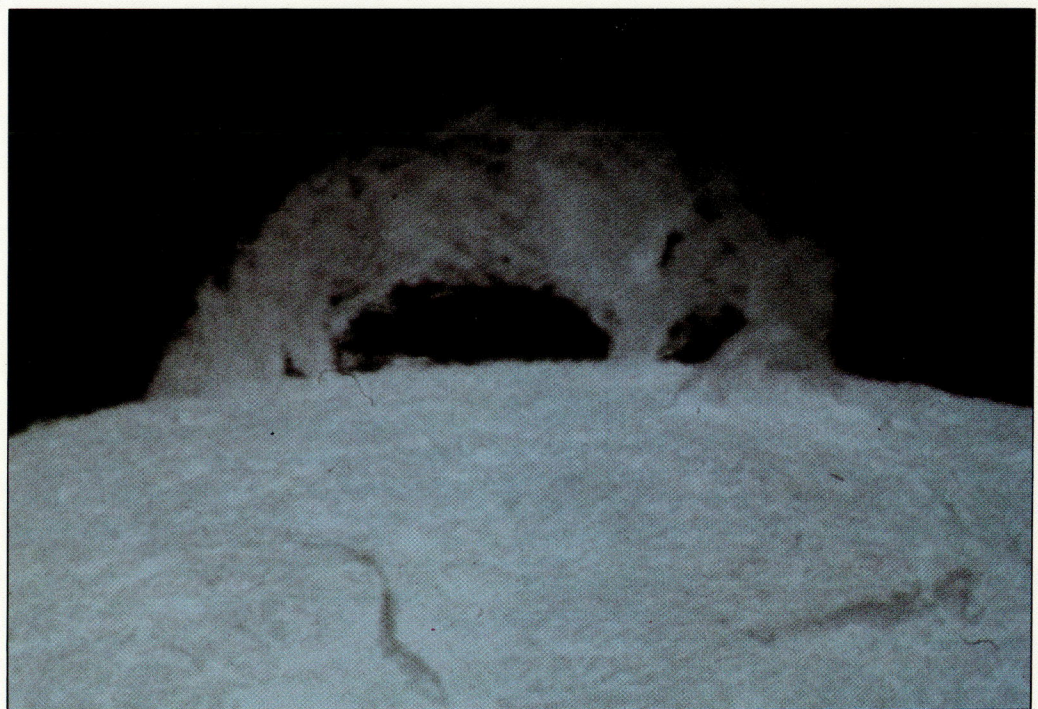

CHRONOLOGY

	Periods/Epoch (Years ago it began)	Development of Oceans and Continents	Development of Plant Life	Development of Animal Life
CENOZOIC ERA — Quaternary Period	**Holocene Epoch** 10 thousand	Glaciers melt and form America's Great Lakes.		Humans hunt and domesticate animals, cultivate plants, and learn to make use of natural resources.
CENOZOIC ERA — Quaternary Period	**Pleistocene Epoch** 1¾ million	The Ice Age.		Modern humans develop. Mammoths, woolly rhinoceroses become extinct.
CENOZOIC ERA — Tertiary Period	**Pliocene Epoch** 14 million	Climate begins to cool.		Appearance of first humans. Sea life resembles that of today.
CENOZOIC ERA — Tertiary Period	**Miocene Epoch** 26 million		Trees and plants begin to resemble those of today.	Apes first appear in Africa and Asia.
CENOZOIC ERA — Tertiary Period	**Oligocene Epoch** 40 million			Primitive apes first appear.
CENOZOIC ERA — Tertiary Period	**Eocene Epoch** 55 million		Fruits, grains, grasses.	Mammals begin to dominate.
CENOZOIC ERA — Tertiary Period	**Palaeocene Epoch** 65 million			Spread of mammals.
MESOZOIC ERA	**Cretaceous Period** 130 million	Alps, Himalaya, and Rocky mountains begin to form.	Flowering plants.	Extinction of dinosaurs.
MESOZOIC ERA	**Jurassic Period** 180 million	Opening of South Atlantic.	Conifers abundant.	First birds. Dinosaurs at largest size.
MESOZOIC ERA	**Triassic Period** 180 million	Sierra Nevada mountains begin to form. Opening of North Atlantic.	Conifers abundant.	Dinosaurs and mammals begin to appear. Fish begin to resemble those ot today.
PALAEOZOIC ERA	**Permian Period** 275 million	End of Panagea.	Conifers begin to appear.	Mass extinction of trilobites. Fish, amphibians, and reptiles are abundant.
PALAEOZOIC ERA	**Carboniferous Period** 345 million	Glaciations.	First mosses and ferns appear.	Trilobites begin to die out. Fish and amphibians plentiful. First reptiles and giant insects begin to appear.
PALAEOZOIC ERA	**Devonian Period** 405 million	Appalachian mountains begin to form. Coal deposits laid down.		Amphibians begin to appear. Sharks, armoured fish, and lungfish.
PALAEOZOIC ERA	**Silurian Period** 435 million		Land plants first appear.	Trilobites, fish, and molluscs common.
PALAEOZOIC ERA	**Ordovician Period** 480 million	Panagea (one continent).	Algae become plentiful.	Trilobites, corals, and shelled animals common. Jawless fish appear.
PALAEOZOIC ERA	**Cambrian Period** 600 million	Glaciation over much of planet.		Trilobites first appear.
	Precambrian Period 4.5 billion	Glaciations. First sedimentary rocks. Formation of the oceans and beginning of continents.	More advanced, multicellular animals. Sexual reproduction. Plants begin to breathe oxygen. Large amounts of oxygen present in atmosphere. Development of photosynthesis. Stromatolites. Bacteria present, living without oxygen.	

INDEX

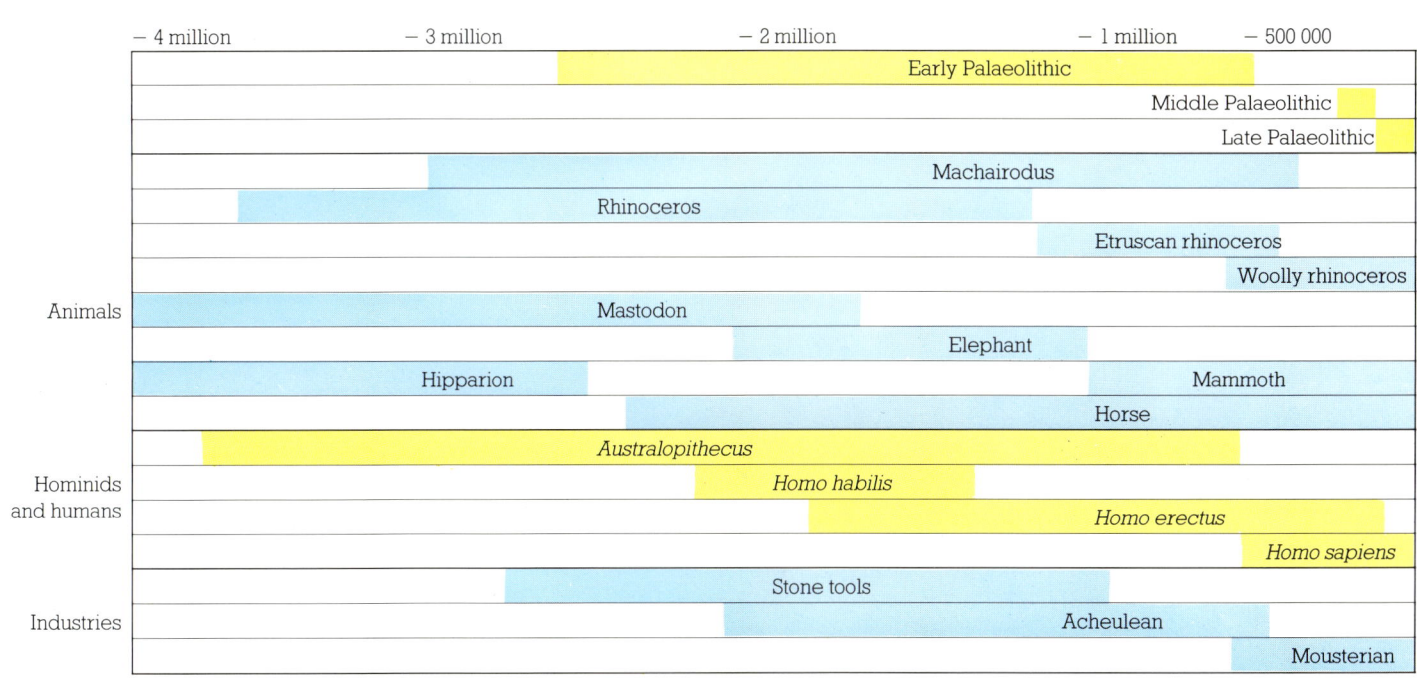

Port Pignot Wimere

La Roche Gélétan

Mauer

Upper Loire

Vallonet

Puig d'en Roca

Aïn Hane

Ternifine

Mansou

Rabat

Reggane